CREATING
Digital
Animations
by Derek Breen

WILEY

CREATING DIGITAL ANIMATIONS

Published by
John Wiley & Sons, Inc.
111 River Street
Hoboken, NJ 07030-5774

www.wiley.com

Copyright © 2016 by John Wiley & Sons, Inc., Hoboken, NJ

Published simultaneously in Canada

No part of this publication may be reproduced, stored in a retrieval system or transmitted in any form or by any means, electronic, mechanical, photocopying, recording, scanning or otherwise, except as permitted under Sections 107 or 108 of the 1976 United States Copyright Act, without the prior written permission of the Publisher. Requests to the Publisher for permission should be addressed to the Permissions Department, John Wiley & Sons, Inc., 111 River Street, Hoboken, NJ 07030, (201) 748-6011, fax (201) 748-6008, or online at http://www.wiley.com/go/permissions.

Trademarks: Wiley, For Dummies, the Dummies Kid logo, Dummies.com, and related trade dress are trademarks or registered trademarks of John Wiley & Sons, Inc. and may not be used without written permission. Scratch is developed by the Lifelong Kindergarten Group at the MIT Media Lab. See www.scratch.mit.edu. Project figures, illustrations and Scratch projects: Copyright © 2015 by Derek Breen. All other trademarks are the property of their respective owners. John Wiley & Sons, Inc. is not associated with any product or vendor mentioned in this book.

LIMIT OF LIABILITY/DISCLAIMER OF WARRANTY: THE PUBLISHER AND THE AUTHOR MAKE NO REPRESENTATIONS OR WARRANTIES WITH RESPECT TO THE ACCURACY OR COMPLETENESS OF THE CONTENTS OF THIS WORK AND SPECIFICALLY DISCLAIM ALL WARRANTIES, INCLUDING WITHOUT LIMITATION WARRANTIES OF FITNESS FOR A PARTICULAR PURPOSE. NO WARRANTY MAY BE CREATED OR EXTENDED BY SALES OR PROMOTIONAL MATERIALS. THE ADVICE AND STRATEGIES CONTAINED HEREIN MAY NOT BE SUITABLE FOR EVERY SITUATION. THIS WORK IS SOLD WITH THE UNDERSTANDING THAT THE PUBLISHER IS NOT ENGAGED IN RENDERING LEGAL, ACCOUNTING, OR OTHER PROFESSIONAL SERVICES. IF PROFESSIONAL ASSISTANCE IS REQUIRED, THE SERVICES OF A COMPETENT PROFESSIONAL PERSON SHOULD BE SOUGHT. NEITHER THE PUBLISHER NOR THE AUTHOR SHALL BE LIABLE FOR DAMAGES ARISING HEREFROM. THE FACT THAT AN ORGANIZATION OR WEBSITE IS REFERRED TO IN THIS WORK AS A CITATION AND/OR A POTENTIAL SOURCE OF FURTHER INFORMATION DOES NOT MEAN THAT THE AUTHOR OR THE PUBLISHER ENDORSES THE INFORMATION THE ORGANIZATION OR WEBSITE MAY PROVIDE OR RECOMMENDATIONS IT MAY MAKE. FURTHER, READERS SHOULD BE AWARE THAT INTERNET WEBSITES LISTED IN THIS WORK MAY HAVE CHANGED OR DISAPPEARED BETWEEN WHEN THIS WORK WAS WRITTEN AND WHEN IT IS READ.

For general information on our other products and services, please contact our Customer Care Department within the U.S. at 877-762-2974, outside the U.S. at 317-572-3993, or fax 317-572-4002. For technical support, please visit www.wiley.com/techsupport.

Wiley publishes in a variety of print and electronic formats and by print-on-demand. Some material included with standard print versions of this book may not be included in e-books or in print-on-demand. If this book refers to media such as a CD or DVD that is not included in the version you purchased, you may download this material at http://booksupport.wiley.com. For more information about Wiley products, visit www.wiley.com.

Library of Congress Control Number: 2016931714

ISBN: 978-1-119-23352-7 (pbk); 978-1-119-23355-8 (ebk); 978-1-119-23354-1 (ebk)

Manufactured in the United States of America

10 9 8 7 6 5 4 3 2 1

CONTENTS

PROJECT 2: ANIMATE GREAT CHARACTERS   *31*

INTRODUCTION

FOR AS LONG AS I CAN REMEMBER, I HAVE WANTED TO TELL MY OWN STORIES WITH ANIMATION. My first project was an animated birthday card for my grandfather. A boat sailed across the screen and then displayed "Happy Birthday." He was blown away, perhaps because this happened over 30 years ago, before computer animation appeared on television or in films.

Today, digital animation is everywhere, but most people think that animating on their own is too hard. Think again! Scratch makes it easy for anybody to get started with animation.

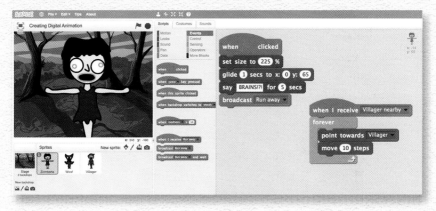

ABOUT SCRATCH

Scratch was created for you. The designers at the MIT Media Lab had several goals:

» Give you powerful software for free

» Make it easy for you to learn

» Allow many different ways for you to use the software

» Enable you to browse, play, and remix other projects

» Enable you to share your projects

» Create an online community where you can learn from one another

Now review that list of six goals. Where does it say, "Force parents or teachers or coaches or kids to buy a big, fat Scratch book"? Nowhere! So why are you still reading? Don't you know you can go to scratch.mit.edu right now and start Scratching?!?

If you are completely new to Scratch, it might be a good idea to start with one of the built-in tutorials. To see them, click the question mark in the top-right corner.

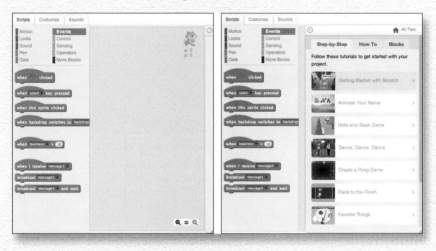

ABOUT THIS BOOK

In this book, you can start with any project. If you have not done much animating inside Scratch, you may find it useful to start with Project 1, which leads you through creating a basic stick figure animation. If you want to design your own cartoon characters, check out Project 2, where I share all kinds of tricks (and you discover that you don't have to be an awesome artist to create great-looking characters).

ICONS USED IN THIS BOOK

The Tip icon marks tips and shortcuts that you can use to make coding easier.

The Warning icon tells you to watch out! It marks important information that may save you from scratching your head a ton.

ACCESS SCRATCH

To use Scratch online visit www.scratch.mit.edu, create an online account, and start Scratching. To use Scratch without creating an account, you will have to download and install the offline version of Scratch (see the upcoming "Use Scratch offline" section).

Technically, you can use the Scratch website without an account, but you will have to save projects to your computer and then upload them each time you visit the Scratch website to continue working on them. With an account, you can save files online and share projects with other Scratch users.

CREATE ONLINE ACCOUNT

Go ahead and start Scratch! Turn on your computer, open a web browser, and visit scratch.mit.edu. If you already have a Scratch account, click the Sign In button in the top-right corner of the page. If you do not have an account, click the Join Scratch button and fill in the brief online form. If you are under 13 or do not have an email account, please ask an adult to help you create an account (or skip ahead to the upcoming "Use Scratch offline" section).

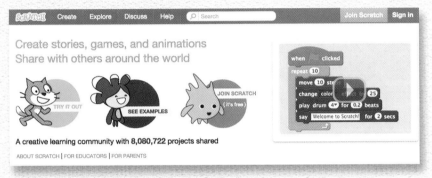

To run Scratch online, you need a relatively recent web browser (Chrome 35 or later, Firefox 31 or later, or Internet Explorer 8 or later) with Adobe Flash Player version 10.2 or later installed. Scratch 2 is designed to support screen sizes 1024 x 768 or larger.

USE SCRATCH OFFLINE

You can install the Scratch 2 Offline Editor to work on projects without a Scratch user account. After Scratch 2 is installed, you will not need an Internet connection to work on projects. This version will work on Mac, Windows, and some versions of Linux (32 bit). Visit www.scratch.mit.edu/scratch2download to download and install Adobe Air (required to run Scratch offline) and the Scratch 2 Offline Editor.

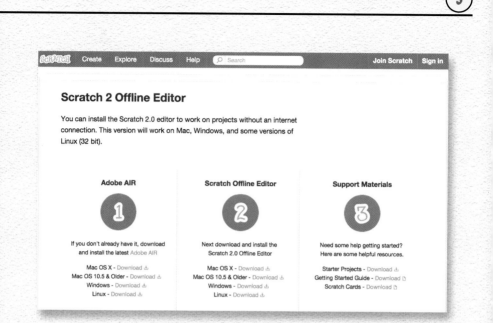

Okay ladies and gentlemen, let's get Scratching!

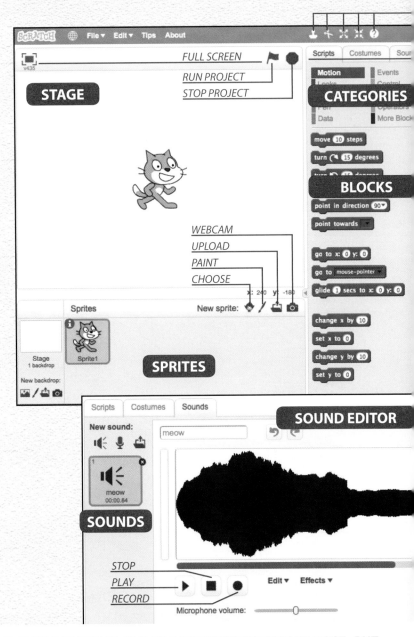

THE SCRATCH INTERFACE CAN BE A BIT INTIMIDATING AT FIRST. BUT IT SHOULD BE PRETTY FAMILIAR BY THE TIME YOU FINISH YOUR FIRST PROJECT.

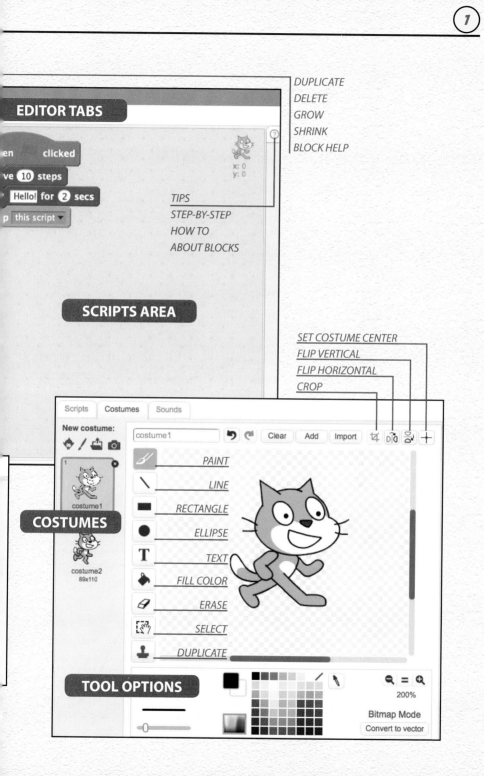

EDITOR TABS

DUPLICATE
DELETE
GROW
SHRINK
BLOCK HELP

en   clicked

ve 10 steps

Hello! for 2 secs

p this script ▾

x: 0
y: 0

TIPS
STEP-BY-STEP
HOW TO
ABOUT BLOCKS

SCRIPTS AREA

SET COSTUME CENTER
FLIP VERTICAL
FLIP HORIZONTAL
CROP

Scripts   Costumes   Sounds

New costume:

costume1   Clear   Add   Import

1
costume1

PAINT
LINE
RECTANGLE
ELLIPSE
T   TEXT
FILL COLOR
ERASE
SELECT
DUPLICATE

COSTUMES

costume2
89x110

TOOL OPTIONS

Q = Q
200%

Bitmap Mode
Convert to vector

PROJECT 1 ANIMATION ESSENTIALS

THIS IS WHERE I AM SUPPOSED TO TALK ABOUT THE HISTORY OF ANIMATION. And then describe all the different kinds and give a bunch of examples and . . . (yawn) . . . No thanks! Wouldn't you rather start animating right now?

In this project, you begin by telling a short story with one of the simplest forms of animation: stick figures. An obvious advantage of stick figures is that they are almost as easy to animate as they are to draw.

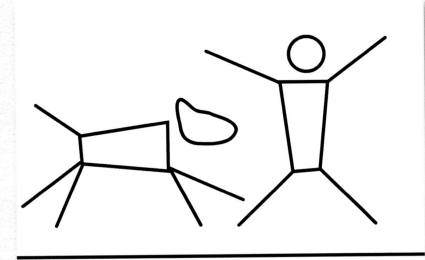

DRAW YOUR FIRST CHARACTER

Go ahead and start drawing! Just kidding. Of course you must create a project before you can draw anything.

CREATE PROJECT

1 Go to scratch.mit.edu or open the Scratch 2 Offline Editor.

2 If you are online, click Create. If offline, choose File ⇨ New.

3 Name your project. (Online, select the title and type Stick Figure Animation. **Offline, choose File ⇨ Save As and type** Stick Figure Animation.)

4 Delete the cat. (Shift-click and select Delete.)

DRAW BODY PARTS

For your stick figure, you need a circle for a head, a rectangle for a body, and lines for arms and legs. Initially, drawing the parts separately might be easier.

1 Click the Paint New Sprite icon.

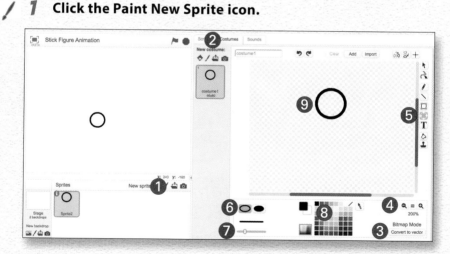

2 Click the Costumes tab.

Convert to vector **3** **Click the Convert to Vector button (bottom-right corner of the Paint Editor).**

4 **Click the Zoom In button one time for 200% scale.**

This scale makes it easier to work on your character.

5 **Click the Ellipse tool.**

6 **Click the Outline option to the left of the color swatches.**

7 **Drag the Line Width slider to adjust the line thickness.**

8 **Choose the black color swatch.**

9 **Click and drag to draw a small, hollow head.**

Hold down the Shift key to draw a perfect circle.

10 **Use the Rectangle tool to draw a hollow body.**

11 **Use the Line tool to draw the arms and legs.**

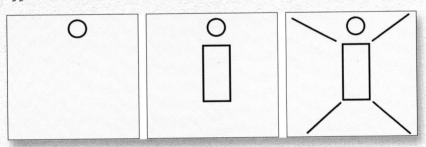

I would never want to animate a stick figure in Bitmap mode because I would miss out on using one of the most valuable tools: the Reshape tool.

SCULPT THE BODY WITH THE RESHAPE TOOL

Here's how to make the rectangle more of a human shape and connect the arms and legs:

1 **Click the Reshape tool and then click the body outline.**

2 **Click and drag each corner of the body into a new position.**

3 **Click and drag the end of each arm onto the top body corners where the shoulders would be.**

4 **Click and drag the top of each leg onto the bottom body corners.**

See how the Reshape tool helps you modify your stick figure easily? Because you have been working zoomed in to 200% on the Paint Editor canvas, check to see how your figure looks on the Stage (the large area to the left of the Paint Editor). My lines appear a bit too thin.

ADJUST THE THICKNESS OF MULTIPLE LINES

Fortunately, there is a quick way to adjust all the lines that make up your vector sprite:

1 **Click the Select tool.**

2 **Click and drag across the entire figure on the Paint Editor canvas to select all the lines.**

3 **Use the Line Width slider to increase the line thickness.**

4 **Check the sprite on the Stage to determine the best thickness for your figure.**

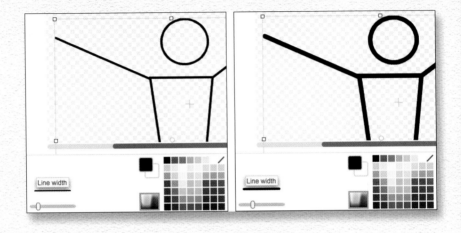

ANIMATE THE STICK FIGURE

In Scratch, you can animate your character in two ways: by changing its position on the Stage or by switching costumes in a sprite. Say you want your character to do a few jumping jacks; you already have the arms-and-legs-out pose, so you need to create just the arms-and-legs-in pose.

1 Shift-click Costume1 and select Duplicate.

2 Select the Reshape tool, click the left arm, and then click and drag the hand end down.

3 Repeat Step 2 for the other arm and both legs.

4 Click back and forth between Costume1 and Costume2 to see the change.

When I alternate clicking between Costume1 and Costume2, something is wrong. Instead of doing jumping jacks, my character looks like he is lying down and making snow angels.

When you do a jumping jack, you don't just wave your arms and your legs. Your body moves, too. How do you show the entire body moving? You need something that remains stationary while the body moves up and down.

DRAW A SIMPLE BACKDROP

I hope you are ready for this. Draw a straight line! Just one line representing the ground will make a big difference. Trust me. I suggest using Vector mode to keep your graphics consistent and to modify the backdrop later, if you desire.

1 **Click the Stage icon to the left of your stick figure sprite.**

vert to vector **2** **Click the Convert to Vector button.**

3 **Use the Line tool to draw a black line all the way across the Paint Editor canvas near the bottom of the window. Hold down the Shift key to avoid drawing a slanted line.**

4 If necessary, use the Line Width slider to adjust the line thickness the way you did for your stick figure.

Compare your figure and the new line on the Stage.

ADJUST MOVEMENT AGAINST THE BACKDROP

In each jumping jack pose, the feet should be on the ground. You can treat the bottom of the Paint Editor canvas as the ground for all your costumes to make them consistent.

1 Click your stick figure sprite and then click Costume1 on the Scripts tab.

2 Use the Select tool to click and drag over the entire figure.

3 Click the Down Arrow key on your keyboard several times until the stick figure's feet line up with the bottom of the Paint Editor canvas.

4 If necessary, use the Reshape tool to align the bottom of each leg with the bottom of the window.

5 Repeat Steps 1–4 for Costume2.

Why use the Down Arrow key when you can just click and drag? Because you don't want to move the sprite left or right accidentally (which would make the animation appear jittery).

Return to the Stage, click your stick figure, and then drag it so the bottom of each leg aligns with the ground. If you alternate between Costume1 and Costume2, the feet should now remain on the ground.

But something is still missing. Stand up and do a few jumping jacks. Seriously! One thing you need to do as an animator is act out each movement.

Do your feet stay in contact with the floor the entire time? Of course not. Why do they call them *jumping* jacks? Because you jump up!

PUTTING THE JUMP IN JACKS

Right now, if you alternate costumes, it's like the feet just slide across the floor. You need to add a pose between Costume1 and Costume2 with the arms and legs midway between the other poses and the body above the ground. This also is a good time to rename the costumes so you don't get confused.

1 **Click Costume1, select the costume name, and then type** Arms Up.

2 **Click Costume2 and rename it** Arms Down.

3 **Shift-click the Arms Up costume and select Duplicate.**

4 **Click and drag the new costume up so it comes between Arms Up and Arms Down.**

5 **Rename the middle costume** Arms Mid.

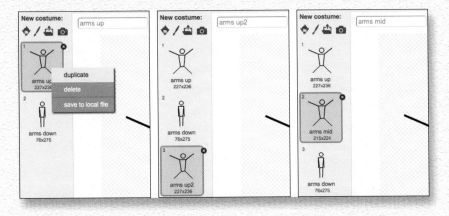

Since the feet are at the bottom of the canvas, you need to select and move the entire figure up before repositioning the legs:

1 Click the Select tool.

2 Click and drag over the entire stick figure to select all the body parts.

3 Click the Up Arrow key 50 times.

4 Use the Reshape tool to drag the ends of the arms and legs closer together.

The bottom of the legs should remain above the floor for the jump. If you want more than one jumping jack, use code to save time.

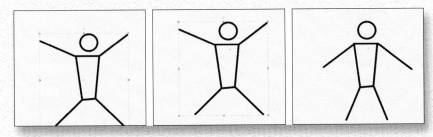

ANIMATE WITH CODE BLOCKS

You start by creating a loop, which will allow you to repeat part of your animation as many times as you want. For ten jumping jacks, follow these steps:

1 **Click the Scripts tab for *Sprite1*.**

2 **Drag the following blocks into the Scripts Area and change the values to match:**

```
when      clicked
switch costume to  arms down ▾
switch costume to  arms mid ▾
switch costume to  arms up ▾
```

If you click the Green Flag button to test your code, what happens? Nothing *appears* to happen because the costume changes appear so fast you can't see them. You need to add WAIT blocks between the SWITCH COSTUME blocks to slow down the change enough for you to see it. The default of 1 second is too long, so try changing the value to **.25** (for a quarter of a second) for each block:

```
when      clicked
switch costume to  arms down ▾
wait .25 secs
switch costume to  arms mid ▾
wait .25 secs
switch costume to  arms up ▾
wait .25 secs
```

Now when you click the Green Flag button, you should be able to see the costume changes. If you want your figure to do ten jumping jacks, you could drag a whole lot more blocks over or add just one REPEAT block:

```
when   clicked
repeat 10
    switch costume to arms down ▾
    wait .25 secs
    switch costume to arms mid ▾
    wait .25 secs
    switch costume to arms up ▾
    wait .25 secs
```

Your stick figure should do ten jumping jacks, but they don't look right. Can you spot what is missing in the code? The figure starts in the arms down position, switches to arms mid, then arms up, and then skips back to arms down for the repeat. You need to add another arms mid position to smooth the animation between each repeat. And each SWITCH COSTUME needs a WAIT block, too:

```
when   clicked
repeat 10
    switch costume to arms down ▾
    wait .25 secs
    switch costume to arms mid ▾
    wait .25 secs
    switch costume to arms up ▾
    wait .25 secs
    switch costume to arms mid ▾
    wait .25 secs
```

Click the Green Flag button and you should now see all the costume changes through ten jumping jacks. But there's still one more problem. When you do jumping jacks, don't you pause a moment in both your arms up and arms down positions? There should be a longer WAIT after those poses, right? I spent a few minutes trying different WAIT values and found that these ones work best:

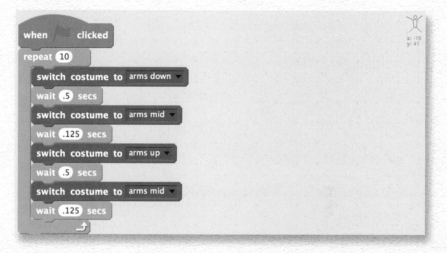

The jumping jacks should look much better when you click the Green Flag button. But did you notice how it freezes on the last jumping jack mid-jump? You need one more SWITCH COSTUME block *after* the REPEAT block to bring your figure back to the upright position:

Maybe I am in too much of a rush, but I don't want to have to sit through ten jumping jacks every time I make a change in my code. I usually use a smaller number while coding and then raise the value when I am happy with how the animation looks.

BRING HUMOR TO YOUR ANIMATION

If you search YouTube or other online video sites, you can find thousands of hilarious stick figure animations. What do they all have in common? Like any story, your animation should have a beginning, a middle, and an end. But what makes most of them funny? Usually, it's the element of surprise!

I know nothing is surprising about a stick figure who does ten jumping jacks. If you want to make it funny, what could you add to surprise the audience? Right now, the jumping jacks are like a story that's just a middle (no beginning or ending).

To transform this scene into a funny story, you need to answer two questions:

1 **Why is a stick figure doing jumping jacks?**

2 **What could prevent the stick figure from finishing jumping jacks?**

Watch just about any humorous scene and you will notice a character who really wants something and an obstacle preventing the character from getting it. In the Pixar movie *Up*, a grumpy old man wants to get away from everybody, so he straps all these balloons on his house and then takes off. What goes wrong? An annoying little Boy Scout flies off with him.

Maybe you need a second character, like the little boy in *Up*, or Batman in *The Lego Movie*, or Donkey in the *Shrek* movies, or the dog in . . . that's it! Let's give our stick person a stick pet! A dog that prevents him from finishing his morning exercises!

ADD STICK MAN'S BEST FRIEND

Here's another of my favorite Scratch stick-figure animation tricks. Instead of drawing a new character, you can duplicate your first character and reassemble the body parts (a bit like

Dr. Frankenstein). This way, you make sure the characters are the right scale and look good together:

1 **Shift-click Sprite1 and choose Duplicate.**

2 **To rename the two sprites, choose Info and then change the names.**

I'll call the first sprite *Sticky* and the second sprite *Woof*.

3 **Click the Back button to exit Info view.**

You should now have two sprites. Click the *Woof* sprite's icon, go to the Costumes tab, and delete all but the first costume by clicking the small X on each costume's icon. The first costume will be the basis for the new character.

MODIFY PARTS TO CREATE A NEW CHARACTER

You will use the Select tool to rotate the body and drag the other body parts into position. Then use the Reshape tool to sculpt the dog's head:

1 **Click the Select tool.**

2 **Click the body shape.**

3 **Click the rotate handle (the small circle above the selected shape) and drag to rotate the body into a horizontal position.**

4 **Click and drag the arms and legs into position.**

5 **Click the Reshape tool.**

6 **Click the head, and then click and drag the control points to sculpt the head into more of a dog head shape.**

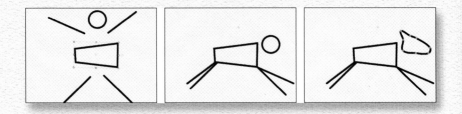

DEVELOP YOUR HUMOROUS STORY

The dog will be the obstacle to *Sticky* finishing his morning exercise, but how can you start the story? Why is *Sticky* exercising? I can think of all kinds of reasons, but what would be a simple one that you could show quickly (so you do not have to spend hours animating)? What if *Sticky* puts up a new poster of muscle stick man? It might be funny to see a skinny stick figure walk across the Stage and put up a poster of a stick figure with crazy muscles.

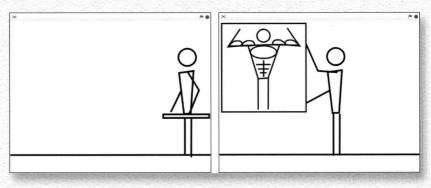

Then *Sticky* starts doing jumping jacks, but the dog runs over and nags him. *Sticky* ignores the dog until it jumps up and tears part of the poster. Then *Sticky* ends up chasing the dog for so long, he ends up with huge leg muscles instead of muscular arms, chest, and six-pack abs. That *could* be funny.

How could you make it easier? What if the poster is already on the wall when *Sticky* enters? The dog could be there, too. Then you just need to have the man enter the scene.

WALK LIKE A MAN

Let's get *Sticky* onto the Stage as fast as possible, okay? Wait, he's already on the Stage. Get him off there!

1 Hide *Woof* for now by Shift-clicking the sprite and selecting Hide.

2 Select *Sticky* and change his costume to Arms Down.

3 Click and drag *Sticky* to the far-right side of the Stage.

You want *Sticky* to walk onto the Stage before doing the jumping jacks, so the new code needs to go between WHEN GREEN FLAG CLICKED and the REPEAT block. Snap the following code blocks right under WHEN GREEN FLAG CLICKED and change the values to match:

What if you add a sleeping pose to *Woof* and have the dog wake up when the man begins exercising?

ROTATE PARTS WITH THE SELECT TOOL

To preserve the length of lines while rotating, use the Select tool. With vector shapes, you can even change the point around which they rotate by following these steps.

1 **Shift-click the *Woof* icon and select Show.**

2 **Click *Woof* to select the sprite and then click the Costumes tab.**

3 **Shift-click the costume and select Duplicate (in case you want to use the original pose later).**

4 **Click to select the new costume and rename it** sleeping.

5 **Click the Select tool and click one of the hind legs.**

6 **Shift-click the small circle in the center of the selection square and then drag it to the end of the leg where it meets the dog's hip.**

7 **Move your cursor to the circle outside the box until it turns into a circular arrow.**

8 **Click and drag the circular arrow to rotate the leg forward until it is under the dog's body.**

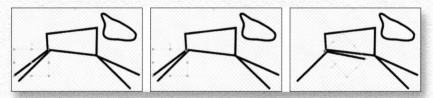

Rotate the remaining three legs using the same steps, lower the head and the tail to look more like those of a sleeping dog, and then click and drag the sprite into position on the left side of the Stage.

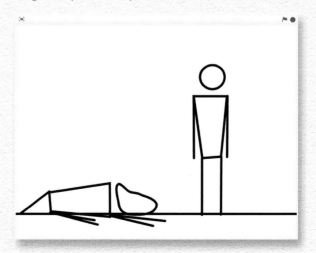

ANIMATE THE DOG

I think it's finally time to bring the dog to life, don't you? Design an awake costume for *Woof:*

1 **Shift-click *Woof's* sleeping costume and choose Duplicate.**

2 **Rename the costume** Wake.

3 **Click the Select tool.**

4 **Click and drag the dog's head up a bit (or you can use the Up Arrow key for a more precise movement).**

5 **Click and drag to rotate the tail up.**

ADD CODE TO ANIMATE THE STICK DOG

Timing is essential in animation, especially when you have two or more characters interacting. Can you figure out how many seconds the dog should wait until waking up? Look back at the code on *Sticky:* three seconds to glide in and then a one-second pause before starting the jumping jacks. So the dog should wait about five seconds, right?

1 **Click the Scripts tab.**

2 **If you duplicated the stick figure sprite to make the dog as I did, the tab will already contain jumping jack code. Shift-click the WHEN GREEN FLAG CLICKED block and choose Delete.**

3 **Drag the following code blocks to the Scripts Area and change the values to match:**

```
when    clicked
switch costume to  sleep ▼
wait 5 secs
switch costume to  wake ▼
```

Click the Green Flag button and the dog should sleep for five seconds, and then appear to wake up by lifting its head and tail. What might the dog do next? When I enter a room that has a dog, it usually starts wagging its tail.

ANIMATE TAIL WAGGING

For a quick tail wag, duplicate the Wake costume, rename the new costume **Wag**, and use the Select tool to rotate the tail.

Use a REPEAT block to switch between the Wake and Wag costumes. I think we also should add a two-second delay between the dog first waking and then wagging its tail. (Surely dogs need a few seconds between waking and showing excitement.)

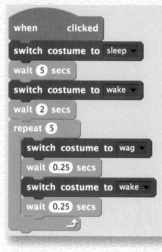

TALK LIKE A MAN

The characters are stick figures, so I think it works best to "stick" (pretty hilarious, right?) to speech bubbles, rather than recorded sounds and voices. (You use digital audio in Project 4.) You could draw a speech bubble into a new costume or make a separate sprite, but I find using the SAY blocks easier.

I want my figure to speak WHILE doing jumping jacks. If I put a SAY block inside the REPEAT block, *Sticky* will keep saying the same thing over and over until the last jumping jack is finished.

What is a poor little animator to do?

Scratch can have different chunks of code running at the same time on different sprites and even within the same sprite. This means you can keep your current gliding and jumping jacks code blocks on the stick figure, add a second WHEN GREEN FLAG

CLICKED block, and then use some more WAIT blocks to time your speaking:

1 **Click the *Sticky* sprite icon and then click the Scripts tab.**

2 **Drag the new blocks into the Scripts Area to the right of the current set of blocks:**

3 **Click inside each SAY block and replace *Hello!* with whatever you want your stick figure to say (unless you want your character to say, "Hello . . . Hello!").**

I will have my guy say, "Go back to sleep" and then "Let me finish!"

```
when  clicked                    when  clicked                    x: 100
switch costume to arms down ▼    wait 8 secs                       y: 38
go to x: 260 y: 38               say Go back to sleep. for 2 secs
glide 3 secs to x: 100 y: 38     say Let me finish! for 2 secs
```

I am going to let you finish the animation on your own. You have all the tools and techniques you need to make *Woof* sit up, bark, do jumping jacks, and attack *Sticky*. The remaining choices are more about the story. What is the story you want to tell?

PROJECT 2 ANIMATE GREAT CHARACTERS

ENOUGH WITH STICK PEOPLE! In this project, you create a unique cast of characters by using vector-drawing tools and then you learn a few design techniques to help bring them to life.

KEEP IT SIMPLE, STUPID

When I was younger, I learned that *KISS* means more than just smacking your lips into somebody. It can stand for *Keep It Simple, Stupid.* The more complex your characters are, the harder it is to animate them. So keep your character design simple, dummy!

If your goal is to create simple characters, doesn't it make sense to begin with a few simple shapes? When designing a new character, I often start with just three circles:

What do you see? A face, right? Now, what happens if I move the eyes around?

Although the three circles are the same size, placing the eyes in different locations already begins to suggest three different characters. Add two smaller circles to each set of eyes . . .

. . . draw a simple line for a mouth . . .

. . . and then fill each face with a different color:

Wow, I don't know what you see, but I see a zombie, a person, and a werewolf!

To keep it simple, I will create a story that involves these three characters and explore ways to bring the characters and their world to life.

GETTING A HEAD START

Before starting, take a moment to think about the story you want to tell and the characters who would be the most fun to bring to life. If you don't have a good idea yet, don't worry, you can start messing around with a few characters and see where they lead you.

CREATE A NEW PROJECT

1 **Go to** scratch.mit.edu **or open the Scratch 2 Offline Editor.**

2 **If you are online, click Create. If offline, choose File ⇨ New.**

3 **Name your project. (Online, select the title and type** Animation Characters. **Offline, choose File ⇨ Save As and type** Animation Characters.**)**

4 **Delete the cat!**

PAINT A NEW SPRITE

1 **Click the Paint New Sprite icon.**

2 **Click the Costumes tab.**

Convert to vector | 3 **Click the Convert to Vector button.**

4 **Click the Ellipse tool.**

5 **Click the Outline option.**

6 **Choose the black color swatch.**

7 **Click and drag to draw a head and two eyes.**

You can hold down the Shift key to draw a perfect circle.

8 **Draw two more ellipses for eye pupils.**

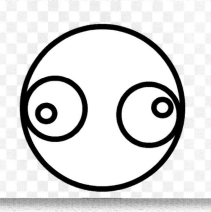

If you want your eyes to be exactly the same size, use the Duplicate tool to make exact copies.

Is your character beginning to emerge? If not, perhaps a bit of hair will help.

QUICK HAIRSTYLING

You can draw hair with the Pencil tool or sculpt it by using the Reshape tool on an ellipse or a rectangle. I will combine techniques to get a unique hairstyle for my zombie:

1 **Click the Ellipse tool.**

2 **Click the Solid option.**

3 **Choose a color swatch for your hair color.**

4 **Click and drag right over your character's face.**

5 **Shift-click the Back a Layer button to send the hair to the bottom layer (behind the head and eyes).**

6 **Click the Reshape tool.**

7 **Click the hair to select it.**

8 **Click and drag control points to style your hair.**

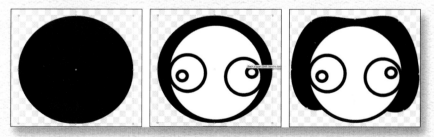

The Pencil tool is better at drawing jagged shapes, like zombie hair bangs!

1 **Click the Pencil tool.**

2 **Choose a color swatch.**

3 Click and drag to start drawing.

4 Drag the pencil back to the starting point to create a closed shape that can be filled with color.

5 Click the Color a Shape tool and then click inside the new shape to fill it.

Using the Pencil tool generally creates many more control points than the Line, Ellipse, or Rectangle tools do. You can use the Reshape tool to smooth lines, which reduces the number of points and makes sculpting shapes and animating them later easier. Click any vector shape with the Reshape tool and the Smooth button will appear above the Line Width slider.

Smooth

OPEN WIDE

What fun is a zombie without a mouth to bite off your arm or munch on your brains? Animating later will be easier if you begin with an open mouth, so draw an ellipse in the open position first:

1 Click the Ellipse tool to draw the mouth open.

2 Click the Reshape tool, click the mouth one time, and then click and drag points into the shape you want.

3 Click the Color a Shape tool, choose a lip color, and then click the edge of the mouth to create lips.

4 Click the Select tool, click the mouth, and then use the Line Width slider to adjust the line thickness.

GIVE 'EM A NOSE JOB

Although some zombies may have lost a nose in their travels, I think my little ghoul could use a petite schnoz. Use the Pencil tool to draw the nose on yours and then use the Reshape tool to smooth it.

Nose placement can affect your character as much as the location of the eyes and mouth, so you might want to try a few positions before you lock in your face for all eternity.

A LITTLE BODY WORK

Having the body, arms, and legs as separate objects makes characters easier to animate.

1 Click the Ellipse tool, choose your outline color, and then draw an oval the approximate size you want for the body.

I'll choose classic black for my outline color.

2 Click the Color a Shape tool, choose a color for the character's shirt or dress, and then click inside the initial body shape.

3 Click the Reshape tool, click the body to select it, and then click and drag points into the shape that looks best to you.

ADD SIMPLE LEGS

You can use the Rectangle tool to draw the legs together, use the Reshape tool to taper them at the ankles, and then fill them in with the pants, tights, or zombie skin color of your choice.

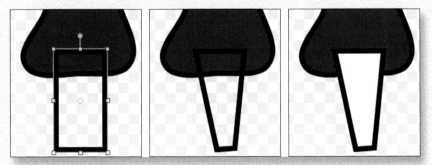

Something doesn't look right. Oh yeah! I don't want the zombie's dress to be too short. Shift-click the Back a Layer button so the legs appear behind the body. Then draw an ellipse and reshape it into shoes.

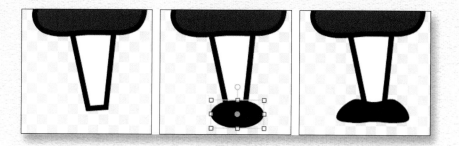

ARMING YOUR CHARACTERS

Although you can get away with combining legs, your character should have two arms, right? You can follow the lazy animator way by drawing the left arm and then using the ole' one-two punch of duplicate and flip.

1 Use the Ellipse tool to draw the left arm.

2 Use the Reshape tool to refine the shape.

3 Fill the shape with skin color.

I'll choose zombie-white.

4 Click the Duplicate tool, click the arm, and then drag the copy to the other side.

5 Click the Flip Left-Right button.

6 Click the Select tool and then drag the arm into the correct position.

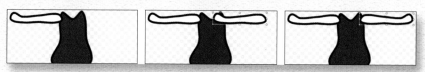

Oops, I just noticed my character is missing a neck! Why not duplicate the leg shape and flip it vertically?

1 Click the Duplicate tool, click the legs, and then drag the new legs to where the neck should be.

2 Click the Flip Up-Down button.

3 Shift-click the Back a Layer button.

APPLY FINISHING TOUCHES

Can you add details to make your character stand out? I used the Reshape button to give the bottom of my zombie dress more of a torn look and decided to go with bluish skin and dull gray pupils.

I know exactly what you are thinking: "That is so much work. How the heck will I be able to finish the other characters for my animation?"

IT'S OKAY TO CLONE SCRATCH PEOPLE

The same way you duplicated body parts, you can now duplicate your entire character and simply apply a few changes to make a completely different person for your animation.

1 **Shift-click your first character sprite on the Stage and choose Duplicate.**

2 **Shift-click the first sprite again, click the Info button, and then rename the character.**

I will call my zombie girl *Zomberta*.

3 **Rename the duplicate sprite.**

This will be my werewolf, so I will name it *Werewoof*.

FROM DEAD SKIN TO FURRY BEAST

Some of the quickest ways to change a character are to swap colors, change the hair shape, and give the face a makeover:

1 **Click the Color a Shape tool, choose your color, and then click inside the shapes you want to change.**

2. **Click the Select tool, and then click and drag the eyes and pupils into new positions.**

3. **Click the Reshape tool, click each shape you want to modify, and then click and drag the points to create your character's new appearance.**

4. **Use the Reshape tool to change the eye and hair shapes.**

Well, _Werewoof_ is definitely headed in the right direction. But with that empty mouth, it's hardly a ferocious beast.

FANGS MAKE THE BEAST

When drawing detailed shapes, such as sharp teeth, either zoom in or draw the shape large and then shrink it to size:

1 **Click the Line tool.**

2 **Click the Outline option.**

3 **Click the black color swatch.**

4 **Click and drag to draw one side of fangs.**

5 **Click back on first point to close the shape.**

6 **Click the Color a Shape tool, click the white swatch, and then click inside the shape.**

7 **Click the Duplicate tool, click the first set of fangs, and then drag them to the other side of the snout.**

8 **Click the Flip Left-Right button to flip the fangs.**

9 **Use the Select tool to drag the fangs into position.**

10 **Use the Reshape tool to adjust the mouth to fit the new snappers.**

Ah, the fangs make my character much more ferocious, but he kinda looks like he's wearing a furry dress. Well, who says *Werewoof* is a boy? Okay, then *she* looks like she's wearing a furry dress!

UNDRESS THE BEAST

Before you delete the dress (or some other body part), take a moment to think about whether it could serve another purpose. It occurs to me that if I resize the dress and move it up to the shoulders, it could look more like fur:

1 Click the Select tool, click the dress, and then drag the bottom side up to make it shorter.

2 Click and drag the shape up to the shoulder area.

3 Click the Ellipse tool and then draw a new body shape.

4 Click the Reshape tool, click the body, and then drag the points to make ribs.

5 Click the Select tool, click the legs shape, and then resize the legs to fit.

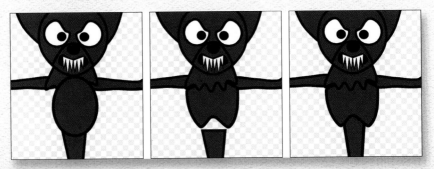

STRIKE A POSE

I'm satisfied with the shape of my (somewhat cheesy) werewolf, but it looks weird with the arms outstretched in the zombie's pose. Quickly repositioning body parts is one of the reasons we went with Vector mode.

Duplicate a character's costume (Shift-click ⇨ Duplicate) before changing any pose to make returning to the original pose easy.

1 **Click the Select tool and then click the left arm.**

2 **Shift-click the small circle in the center of the selection square and drag it to the shoulder.**

3 **Move your cursor to the small circle above the selection box until it turns into a circular arrow. Then click and drag the circular arrow to rotate the arm.**

4 **Repeat Steps 1–3 for the right arm.**

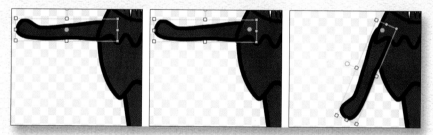

You may have to readjust the center of rotation each time you rotate a body part, even if you moved it before.

ADD FINISHING TOUCHES

Now what would make the werewolf more *werewolfy?* Instead of standing up tall, how about changing it to a crouching position?

1 Click the Reshape tool and then click the legs.

2 Shift-click and drag a new point and curve on each side.

3 Click the Select tool, click the legs, and then drag up.

4 Click the feet and drag them up to the new leg position.

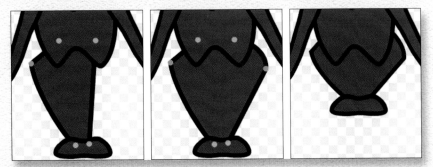

Rotating the arms was not enough. Now that the werewolf is crouching, I want to bend the arms and add some claws! You could draw new claws, but your lazy author will simply duplicate the fangs and reshape them to fit each paw:

1 Click the Reshape tool and then click the left arm.

2 Click and drag points into a bent arm position.

3 Click the Duplicate tool, click one set of fangs, and then drag them to the left paw.

4 Click the Reshape tool, select the claws, and then adjust the points.

5 Repeat Steps 1–4 for the right arm (or duplicate and flip the left arm and claw).

CREATE A THIRD CHARACTER

If you look at the two characters side-by-side, you would hardly guess they came from the same basic figure (unless you did all the work).

I set out to design three unique figures. The one remaining character is the regular person — who should have a lot to worry about in this company.

Decide which sprite is closer in shape to the new character you want to create. *Zomberta* is more like a person than my crouching, snarling werewolf, so I will duplicate her:

1 **Shift-click the sprite you want to copy and then choose Duplicate.**

2 **Shift-click the new sprite, click the Info button, and then change the name.**

I will name my person *Hector*. Why not?

3 **Click the Costumes tab.**

FROM ZOMBIE GIRL TO BLAND BOY

You already transformed one character into another character, so I am going to move quickly this time. I will start by changing the skin and hair colors from zombie girl to ordinary boy. Then I will draw more boyish hair (you can use the Pencil or the old Reshape-on-an-Ellipse technique), reshape the nose, and move the pupils to the middle of his eyes.

I am not saying that anything is wrong with a boy wearing a dress, but I want my character to have a more traditional boyish outfit to go with the story I have in mind. The dress shape is all wrong, so I will delete it, create a new shirt, and then color the legs to look like long pants.

USING THE ADVANCED COLOR PALETTE

Skin color can be a tricky thing to get right. By default, you can choose from only 56 color swatches in the Paint Editor.

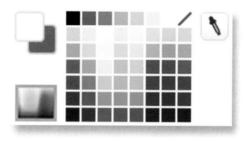

Fortunately, Scratch has a bunch more color options just a click away. Click the Switch Color Palette button at the bottom of the Paint Editor, just to the left of the color swatches, to switch to the Advanced Color Palette.

Click and drag that small circle inside the blended colors until you get the color you want, and then use the Shade slider on the right side to make the color darker or lighter. You can use the Pick Up Color tool (the dropper beside each color palette) to select a color from any object on the Paint Editor canvas. To return to the basic swatches, click the Switch Color Palette button again.

DESIGN CHARACTER CLOTHING

I may want to create a regular girl character later (perhaps showing Zomberta before her zombie transformation) so, before changing the dress, I will duplicate the costume.

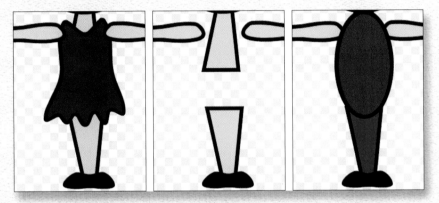

Use the Reshape tool to sculpt the ellipse into a t-shirt. You can click anywhere on the outline to add more points. I will add two points to each shoulder to get the sleeves right.

Now that *Hector's* clothes are complete, I'm no longer happy with how his face looks.

TWEAK FACIAL FEATURES

Use the Reshape and Select tools to experiment with different eyes and noses. It might also help to add eyebrows (tweaking the hair if you need more room for them).

ADD A SET OF TEETH

I am much happier with how the eyes and nose look now. But that mouth is kinda freakin' me out. It looks like somebody knocked out the boy's teeth out. Teeth!

1 **Shift-click the costume and choose Duplicate.**

2 **Click the Color a Shape tool and then choose the white color swatch.**

3 **Click inside the mouth to fill it with white.**

4 **Click the Line tool, choose the black color swatch, and then draw a straight line across the middle of the mouth.**

5 **Click the Reshape tool, click the mouth, and then adjust the shape.**

What an improvement a set of teeth can make to a face! So keep brushing your teeth or you'll end up looking like *Zomberta!*

POSING CLOTHED FIGURES

Moving clothed characters involves a few extra steps. You will need to use the Reshape tool to adjust the shirt after the arms have been rotated. Don't forget to duplicate the costume first in case you want the arms raised later!

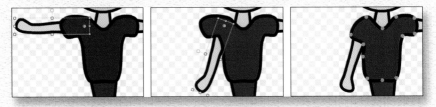

ASSEMBLING YOUR CAST

After following the same steps for the right arm, I wanted to see how the boy looks in comparison to his more gruesome animation mates, so I dragged all three into position on the Stage.

You can spend as much time as you want refining your character designs, but this book is about animation, so let's move on to building your scenes, adding sound, and using special effects to make your cartoons even more memorable.

QUICK CHARACTER IMPROVEMENTS

If you simply must spend a bit more time working on your characters, here are some tips that might help:

» **Compare to other animation characters:** Spend a few minutes reviewing a few of your favorite characters from animated films or shows with a critical eye. What details help distinguish one character from another?

» **Add texture:** Bring your design skills to clothing by adding patterns, shapes, and texture. A few wavy lines can also make for a better hairstyle.

» **Add a more striking pose:** Rather than just having your characters stand around, experiment with more dramatic poses, which helps you express their personalities.

» **Add drama:** Choose a specific scene from the story you have in mind and adjust the characters' poses and expressions to match the tone and mood you want to express.

PROJECT 3 LOCATION, LOCATION, LOCATION

EVERY ANIMATION TAKES PLACE SOMEWHERE. That place might be in a family basement or in the far reaches of outer space, in South America or in South Park, Colorado. The last project walked you through the creation of three different animated characters. Now those characters (or creatures) could use some *immersive scenes* — object-filled locations that grab your senses — to make their lives (and ours) more interesting.

PLANNING ANIMATION SCENES

Every location is going to be either inside or outside, an interior scene or an exterior scene. Let's begin inside.

If you plan to use your characters from the previous project (or from another project you have created), it will be easier to open that project so your characters will be available. If you want to use sprites from the Sprite Library or design new ones later, you can create a new project (and delete the Scratch cat):

1. **Go to scratch.mit.edu or open the Scratch 2 Offline Editor.**

2. **If you are online, browse and open the project you want to copy. If offline, choose File ➪ Open and then select your project.**

3. **If online, click the File menu and choose Save a Copy. If offline, choose File ➪ Save As.**

4. **Name your project as you want. I'll name my project** Animation Backgrounds.

DESIGN AN INTERIOR SCENE

In Project 1, I presented the most basic kind of interior scene, a single horizontal line to indicate the floor. Even for a more complicated scene, determining the intersection of floor and wall is a great place to start.

I recommend that you design your backdrops in Vector mode so you can modify lines and shapes at any time.

1. **Click the Stage icon to the left of the character sprites.**

2. **On the Backdrops tab, click the Convert to Vector button.**

3. **Click the Rectangle tool, choose the black color swatch, and then adjust the line thickness with the Line Width slider to the left of the color palette.**

4. **For your wall, click just off the top-left edge of the Paint Editor canvas, and then click and drag approximately two-thirds of the way down the Paint Editor canvas.**

SHARE SPRITES BETWEEN PROJECTS

What if you want to bring in characters from more than one project or start with a blank project, work on your backdrops, and then bring characters in later? Whether working online or offline, Scratch allows you to export sprites, individual costumes, and backdrops from one project and then import them into another project.

Shift-click a sprite, costume, or backdrop and select Save to Local File.

 Use the Upload Sprite from File or Upload Costume from File button to load your character into a new project.

If you are working online and do not have permission to save files to your computer, fear not! You can use the Scratch Backpack (at the bottom of your Scripts/ Costumes/Sounds page when working online).

You can drag sprites, backdrops, costumes, scripts, and sounds into and out of your Backpack. To date, the offline version of Scratch does not include a Backpack.

5 For your floor, click off the bottom-left edge of the Paint Editor canvas and then drag toward the lower-right corner of the wall.

6 Click the Color a Shape tool, select the color you want to use, and then fill the wall and floor shapes.

I chose dark brown for the floor and light tan for the wall.

Most of the walls in my house have either a window or a door. Windows have the advantage of helping you see the time of day, the weather, or a vicious monster looking for its next meal:

1 Click the Rectangle tool, choose the black color swatch, and drag the Line Width slider to adjust the line thickness.

2 Click and drag to draw the outer part of the window.

3 Click the Line tool, hold down the Shift key, and drag across the middle of the rectangle to divide the shape into two parts.

4 Shift-click and drag down the middle of the top section to indicate two panes of glass in the upper window.

5 Click the Color a Shape tool, choose the light gray color swatch, and click inside the window to fill it with color.

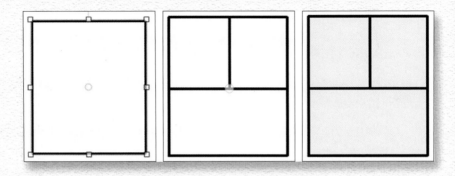

Adding curtains will bring more color into the room and make it obvious that you are inside:

1 Click the Rectangle tool, and then click and drag across the left side of the window.

2 Click the Reshape tool, Shift-click midway down the right side of the rectangle to add a point and a curve, and then drag to the left for an open-curtain look.

3 Click and drag to adjust the top-right and bottom-right points.

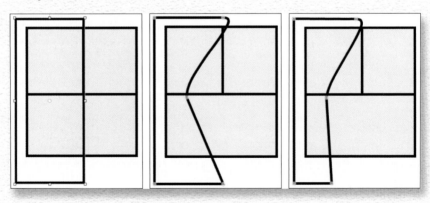

4 Click the Color a Shape tool, choose a curtain color, and then click inside the curtain.

5 Click the Duplicate tool, click the curtain, and then drag the copy to the right side of the window.

6 Click the Flip Left-Right button.

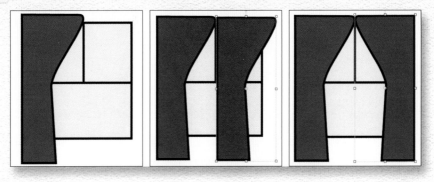

You can use the Reshape tool to adjust the length of the curtain or reveal more of the window.

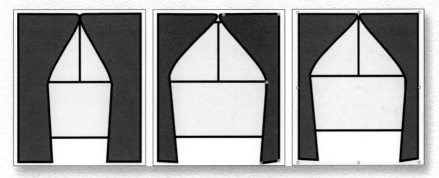

MAKE SCENES MORE IMMERSIVE

What if you want viewers to see objects through a window, or have characters enter and exit through doors or hide behind trees? Instead of putting the walls, windows, floors, and doors all in one backdrop, you can put them in a sprite! Scratch sprites are far more flexible than backdrops; sprites can move behind and in front of each other, move from side-to-side, and get smaller and larger.

CHANGE A BACKDROP INTO A SPRITE

Although you cannot convert a backdrop *into* a sprite, you can drag a backdrop *onto* a sprite, which will become a new *costume* on that sprite:

1 Click the Paint New Sprite button.

2 Click the Stage button (below the actual Stage).

3 On the Backdrops tab, click and drag onto the new sprite the backdrop that includes your window.

4 While you are still on the Backdrops panel, select the plain white backdrop.

If you do not have a backdrop, click the Paint New Backdrop button.

5 Click and drag the new wall sprite into position on the Stage.

DESIGN SEE-THROUGH WINDOWS

You can enable seeing other sprites through windows in a few ways. One way is to delete the color inside the windowpanes, but that won't work here. Can you figure out why? You drew the wall rectangle first and *then* drew the window *over* it. Because it's a vector sprite, each object is on its own layer.

Instead draw a different section of wall to the left, right, top, and bottom edges of the window, remove the glass:

1 Select the wall/floor/window sprite and click the Costumes tab.

2 On the Paint Editor canvas, click anywhere on the wall and then click the Delete key on your keyboard.

3 Click the Color a Shape tool, click the empty color swatch, and then click the glass.

To make a character appear through the window, move the sprite into position, and then send the character to a back layer:

1 On the Stage, click and drag the character(s) to overlap with the window.

2 Click anywhere on the curtain or floor and hold down your mouse or trackpad button for a few seconds to make that sprite move to the front layer.

To keep the window transparent, you will need to draw the wall in four sections and leave a hole around the window:

 **1** **On the Paint Editor canvas, click the Rectangle tool. Then click the Solid option and choose the color of your wall in the Paint Editor.**

2 **Click and drag from just above the top-right corner across the canvas to the right side of the curtain and down to the floor.**

It's okay to overlap the curtain and the floor a bit.

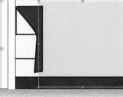 **3** **Hold down the Shift key while you click the Back a Layer button.**

4 **Repeat Steps 2 and 3 for the remaining three sections of the wall. Click off the canvas to ensure the section fills each area.**

After your new wall is filled, you can give viewers a better sense of depth by placing one character inside and placing another outside the window looking in.

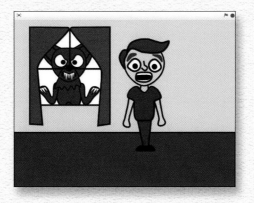

To make the scene more immersive, you can add something inside the room that the character can move in front of and behind. In theater, film, and television, these objects are called *props*.

BUILD YOUR OWN FURNITURE

Nothing quite says "living room" like a big fluffy couch. You can follow along or draw a different prop that fits your room (and your story) better.

The simplest way to draw props is to break them down into smaller parts. Even though most couch cushions are rectangular, it is better to begin with an ellipse and then use the Reshape tool to get the rounded corners right:

1 **Click the Paint New Sprite icon below the Stage.**

2 **Click the Costumes tab and then click the Convert to Vector button.**

3 **Click the Ellipse tool, choose the black color swatch, drag the Line Width slider to adjust the line thickness, and then choose the Outline option.**

4 **Click and drag to draw the first cushion.**

Leave enough room for the arms and two more cushions.

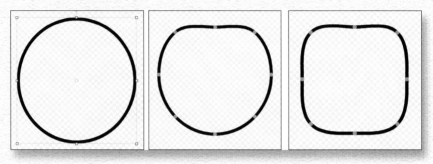

5 Click the Reshape tool, select the cushion, and then click and drag the middle edge points inward to form a rounded rectangle.

6 Click the Color a Shape tool, click the color you think will look good in your room, and then click inside the cushion.

The color should contrast the color of the wall and the character's skin, hair, and clothing.

7 Click the Duplicate tool, click the first cushion, and drag the copy into place beside it. Repeat for the third cushion.

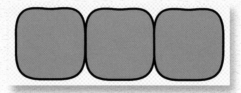

If you hold down the Shift key, you can keep making duplicates of the shape without having to reselect the Duplicate button each time. Release the Shift key before dragging the final copy into place.

8 Click the Select tool and then Shift-click each cushion until all three are selected.

Don't worry about the gaps; you can fill them in later.

9 Click the Group button.

10 Click the Duplicate tool, click the group of cushions, and then drag them to where the seat cushions should be.

11 Click the Select tool and click the bottom-center control point to shorten the group of cushions.

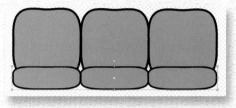

12 Click the Ellipse tool, choose the black color swatch, drag the Line Width slider to adjust the line thickness, and then choose the Outline option.

13 Click and drag to draw an oval where the left couch arm should be.

14 Click the Reshape tool, select the arm, and then click and drag points to sculpt a thick couch arm shape.

15 Click the Color a Shape tool, choose the same color you used for the cushions, and then click inside the arm.

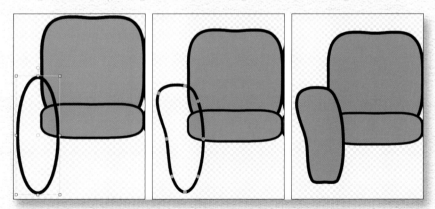

The viewer will not see the other couch arm or the legs in my scene, so I will just draw a rectangle below the cushions, fill it with green, bring the seat cushion group to the front layer (Shift-click the Forward a Layer button). Voila, a living room! But maybe *Hector* should be hiding on the *other* side of the couch, right?

Study your finished scene to make sure sprites do not have too many similar colors. I changed the wall color from tan to a bright yellow after I noticed it was almost the same shade as my character's skin. I also changed the backdrop color to a dark gray so it looks like the werewolf is outside in the dark.

DESIGN AN EXTERIOR SCENE

I haven't used my zombie girl, *Zomberta,* in awhile; she could use a little fresh air. Let's make her first scene her arrival at summer camp. Begin with a new backdrop:

1 **Click the Stage icon to the left of the character sprites.**

Convert to vector **2** **On the Backdrops tab, click the Convert to Vector button in the bottom-right corner.**

3 Click the Rectangle tool, click the Solid option, and then choose a light blue color swatch for the sky.

4 Click just off the top-left edge of the Paint Editor canvas, and then click and drag to approximately halfway down the canvas.

5 Choose a shade of green for the grass, click just off the bottom-left corner of the Paint Editor canvas, and then drag up to the bottom edge of the sky.

It's okay to overlap a bit.

You can make a realistic sky by using a *gradient,* which allows you to blend between two colors.

1 Click the Color a Shape tool.

2 Click the Horizontal Gradient option.

3 Click the white color swatch.

4 Click the Swap Colors button to swap the foreground and background color.

5 Click a sky blue color swatch.

6 Click inside the sky rectangle to replace the flat blue color with the gradient.

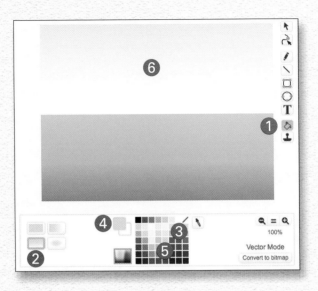

Generally, you will want the sky to be brightest near the horizon and darkest toward the top of the canvas. You can also experiment with gradients on the ground. (I chose a light and darker green.)

Click the Rectangle tool and select a dark gray color swatch. Then click and drag from the horizon (the border between your sky and ground rectangles) down to the bottom of the canvas.

Ewww! That does not look like a road; it ruins the nice sky-over-grass gradient effect and looks more like a flag than a landscape.

DRAW SCENES WITH PERSPECTIVE

By using perspective, you can make some objects appear far away while others appear to be closer to the viewer. Making the top of the road shape narrower will give a better sense of perspective.

 Click the Reshape tool, click the road rectangle to select it, and then click and drag the top points closer together.

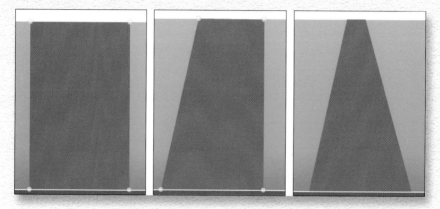

If you are having trouble getting the top corners of the road to line up with the straight horizon or you just want to be lazy like me, try this simple trick. Select the sky rectangle, bring it to the front layer (Shift-click on the Forward a Layer button), and then drag the bottom down to cover the top of the grass and road rectangles.

You can adjust the distance between the left and right corners to give a sense of the road's width and length. The best part is that the road acts as a guide for the rest of the objects in your scene.

Even if your scene is not going to have a road, it might be helpful to draw one initially as a guide for positioning and scaling your objects. I often start with a backdrop like this:

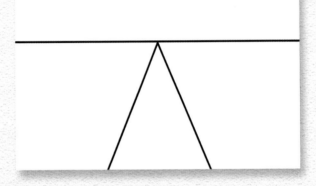

To give the illusion of distance, make the trees smaller and place them closer together farther down the road:

1 **Use the Paint Editor tools to draw your first tree (or other object).**

2 **Use the Duplicate tool to drag copy to align with the road.**

3 **Click the Back a Layer button until it appears behind the first object.**

4 **Use the Shrink tool to make each tree appear smaller than the previous one.**

5 **Use the Select tool to move the tree into place.**

6 **Repeat Steps 2–5 until one side of the road is lined with objects.**

After you have one side of the road complete, you can duplicate the group, flip it horizontally and drag it into place on the other side of the road.

SCALE CHARACTERS INSIDE A SCENE

Another really important element you should use to help lay out your scene is the person or people who will be in it! I've been building roads and planting trees without giving any thought to how large the objects should be in relation to my little zombie.

Unless this is going to be *Attack of the 60-Foot Zombie Girl*, it would be better to figure out how large I want her to appear in the scene, and then leave her on the Stage as a visual reference while adding more objects.

I'm going to delete the trees and the road and start over. This time, I'll add objects in relation to both my road (the driveway leading into the summer camp) and *Zomberta*. Use the same steps that you used for the interior scene: Start with basic shapes and then modify and combine them to make more complex objects.

1 **If your character is still hidden, Shift-click the sprite and select Unhide.**

2 **Use the Grow and Shrink buttons to resize your character.**

The smaller your character, the harder it is to see its expression (not a big deal for zombies but important for most characters).

3 **Use the Reshape tool to adjust the width of your road in relation to your character.**

4 **Begin adding objects in proportion to the road and the character.**

When I am ready to animate *Zomberta* in the scene, I will use perspective to gauge how large she should appear based on how far down the road she goes. Perspective will also dictate when she should be in front of or behind other objects.

There will be plenty of time to improve your immersive scene-building skills (balancing color, placing objects, creating foreground and background) and to play with perspective while you continue with your animation career.

QUICK SCENERY IMPROVEMENTS

Here are a few tips to enhance your scenes:

» **Use reference photographs:** You can use the web or your own camera to grab interior and exterior images. If you want to trace over them, be sure to convert to Vector mode after you import your photo as a sprite or backdrop.

» **Apply more gradients:** Gradients are not just for sky, ground, and road. Try horizontal, vertical, and radial gradients on trees, buildings, or your favorite breakfast cereal. Radial gradients work best on circular objects, and horizontal and vertical gradients work better inside rectangular shapes.

» **Add shadows:** Think about how you might duplicate a sprite, fill it with a dark gray color, and reshape it (like the trees in the first image in this project). Be warned: After you put a shadow on one object, you have to put one on all the other objects or your scene may look incomplete.

» **Consider the weather:** Is it a cloudy day? Rainy? Brainy?

» **Consider the time:** Especially for exterior scenes, it is important to choose whether it is morning, afternoon, or evening.

PROJECT 4 SOUNDS GOOD TO ME

ARE YOU LIKE MY NIECE AND NEPHEW? Half the time that you are supposedly watching television, your eyes are not even on the screen. You're texting somebody with your phone or looking up something on your tablet or playing a game on your laptop or even doing homework. One of the easiest ways to catch your attention is to hit the Mute button on the remote, right? "Hey, I was *watching* that!" This should illustrate how important sound is to conveying a story.

THAT'S WHAT HE SAID

In previous projects, you began thinking about your story, designed some characters, and created an interior and an exterior scene. The next step in the animation process is to add dialogue.

Dialogue is so important to the animation process that voices are recorded before almost any animation begins because synchronizing character animation to sound is easier than trying to fit sound into finished animation. In the animation world, this initial sound recording is the *scratch track*. How perfect is that?

Although this project is about recording and playing audio, there is another way to have your characters speak to one another in Scratch. If you add the SAY block to a character, any text you type in the block will appear in a speech bubble. You can even control how long the speech bubble appears by using a SAY FOR SECONDS block.

WRITE DIALOGUE FOR YOUR CHARACTERS

Okay, don't *hate* me, but even if you are going to provide the voice for all your characters, writing your dialogue before you begin recording is best. You don't have to make it look like a script or anything — just something like this:

```
Hector: Since I got here first, I should get to
    choose which bunk I sleep in.
Zomberta: Brains... brrrraaaaaiiiiinsssss!
Hector: Okaaay... Well, I'd like the top bunk.
Werewoof: Grrrrrrrrrr!
Hector: Does that mean great or what, dog boy?
Werewoof: Aaarrrrgggghhhh!
Hector: Hey, I'm not arguing, I'm just telling you
    how I feel.
Zomberta: Brrrrrr...
Hector: Heh, are you cold, too? Let me get that
    window! I'm more of a DOER than a brainy type.
Werewoof: AAAHHHWWWHHHOOOOOOO!
Hector: Okay, chill out a little, poochie. Boy, you
    could really use a breath mint. What did you have
    for lunch?
Zomberta: Brains!
Hector: Like a grilled brains sandwich or do you eat
    'em right out of the skull? I'm just askin'...
```

I'm not saying you have to type it out as I did; you could scribble some lines on a piece of paper. You just need to put a bit of thought into what your characters are going to say (even if it's only "Grrrrrrrr!") before pressing the Record button. And, if you are going to record anybody else's voice, the actor will need something to read from, right?

RECORD DIALOGUE IN SCRATCH

You should already have created your own Scratch characters and perhaps a background or two for them. Doesn't it make sense to open a project that already has sprites (because it should have your characters, too)?

1 **Go to scratch.mit.edu or open the Scratch 2 Offline Editor.**

2 If you are online, browse and open the project you want to copy. If offline, choose File ⇨ Open and select your project.

3 Name your project. If online, click the File menu and choose Save a Copy. If offline, choose File ⇨ Save As.

I will name my version *Animation Soundtrack*.

4 Delete the cat.

You can add sound to a Scratch project in three ways:

» Choose a sound from the Sound Library.

» Import a sound file (.mp3 or .wav format).

» Record a sound directly in Scratch.

Although the Sound Library has a bunch of music and sound effects to choose from, it has no dialogue.

FIND THE RECORD BUTTON

In the previous projects, you spent most of your time in the Paint Editor. As you may have guessed, in this project you will be spending more time in the Sound Editor.

Click the Sounds tab (to the right of the Costumes tab) to get to the Sound Editor.

Note: If you do not have a microphone connected to your computer or you want to use audio recorded on a different device (such as a phone or a digital recorder), click the Upload Sound from File button and skip ahead to the "Edit Sound Waves" section.

Before you start clicking, recording, and playing, it's important to decide where each sound should go.

In Scratch, sounds are handled the same way as costumes and scripts. Just as each sprite can have several different costumes and code blocks, each sprite can also contain several different sounds. Because my character, *Hector*, has the first line of dialogue, I will select his sprite before recording:

1 **Click the sprite of the character who will be speaking (or growling or moaning), and then click the Sounds tab.**

2 **Shift-click the Pop sound and choose Delete. Or click the X on the Sound icon to delete it.**

By default, each sprite has the *Pop* sound. Unless you are planning to have your character pop (or have it attack a roll of bubble wrap),you need to delete the sound.

3 **Click the Record New Sound button.**

You might think that Scratch would start recording as soon as you click the Record New Sound button. Nope! That button works like the Paint New Costume button; it creates a sound *object* that appears in the New Sound column of the Sound Editor. Like using the Paint tools (Rectangle, Line, and so) to add shapes to a costume, recording adds sound to a sound object.

If you have more than one character in your animation, it is generally a good idea to record each of their lines separately. Later, you will learn how to use code blocks to control when each sound will play.

1 **With the new Recording1 sound object selected, click the Record button.**

If you are using Scratch in a web browser, you may get a message that reads "If you click Allow, you may be recorded." Duh! Of course you may be recorded; you just clicked the Record button! Click Allow to allow Scratch to record.

If the microphone is enabled, the word *Recording* should appear in orange.

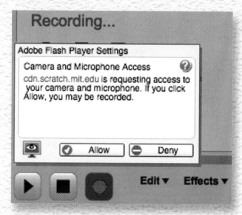

2 **Speak!**

3 **Click the Stop button to end your recording.**

While you are speaking or growling or moaning, a vertical green bar should appear to the left of the recording controls. The bar shows how loud your voice sounds through the microphone. As your voice gets louder, you may see yellow or even red appear near the top of the bar. This means the sound is too loud and may be distorted. You can either lower your voice or adjust the Microphone Volume slider below the Record button. (Move the slider to the left for a real loudmouth or to the right for that friend you are always asking, "Say what?")

EDIT AUDIO CLIPS

Editing your sound recordings is one of the coolest features of Scratch! Imagine if you bribe your big sister to act as the voice of a mad scientist in your cartoon; you go to all the trouble of writing down her dialogue, you hit Record, and she makes a mistake or just pauses too long between two words. Instead of recording the lines again, you can cut out the part you don't want, as easily as selecting and deleting a shape on the Paint Editor canvas.

After you finish recording your sound, something like this should appear in the sound canvas:

That row of black, squiggly shapes is called a *sound wave,* which is a visual version of the sound you just recorded.

▶ Do I *really* need to tell you to click the Play button to hear your recording? Seriously? In case you have trouble finding the button, it's beside Stop and Record.

Now that you have recording and playing sound out of the way, let's get to the cool part: editing sound clips!

When editing a long sound clip, you might find it helpful to expand the Sound Editor. Choose Edit ⇨ Small Stage Layout or click the small, gray triangle between the Stage and the Sound Editor to expand and contract your work area.

TRIM BEGINNING OF SOUND

Start by deleting the extra silence (where the line is completely flat) at the beginning of the sound wave:

1 Select the sprite you recorded audio on, and then click the Sounds tab.

2 If you have more than one sound, click the one you want to edit.

3 Use the horizontal scroll bar to find the beginning of the sound you want to use.

4 Click the sound wave right at the point where the silence *ends* and drag *left,* all the way to the beginning of the sound wave.

5 Below the sound wave, click the Edit menu and choose Delete.

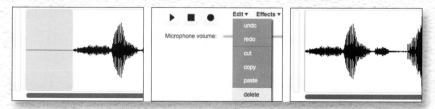

Okay, maybe you don't think it's that cool to delete silence. A bit like deleting nothing, right? But check this out: Each blob represents one word, and the flat lines are the bits of silence in between (unless you talk as fast as my friends in New York City, whose words practically overlap).

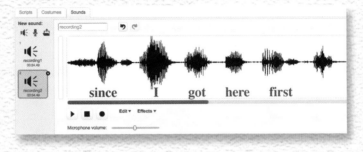

You can delete a word the same way you deleted silence, by clicking and dragging over the word and then choosing Edit ⇨ Delete. The Edit menu also enables you to undo and redo edits, copy part of your audio and paste it somewhere else, and select the entire sound wave.

USE SOUND EDITING EFFECTS

Sound Editor effects allow you to modify the volume of any part of your sound wave, as well as reversing a sound (fun to try out, but not useful for recorded dialogue unless you want a character possessed by a demon).

Try making one of the words in your recording louder:

1 **Click and drag to select the part of the sound wave you want to make louder.**

2 **Below the sound wave, click the Effects menu and choose Louder.**

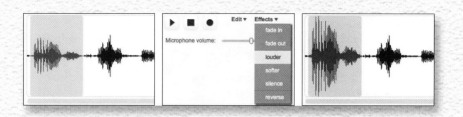

Notice how that part of the sound wave appears taller after the effect is applied. Sound may be invisible in the real world but not inside Scratch!

PLAY SOUND WITH CODE BLOCKS

You know how to play sound in the Sound Editor, but how do you get the sound to play along with the animation? Two code blocks make the recorded dialogue start when the Green Flag button on the Stage is clicked:

1 **Click the sprite of the character for which you recorded dialogue.**

2 **Click the Scripts tab.**

3 **Click the Sound category.**

4 **Drag the PLAY SOUND block *or* the PLAY SOUND UNTIL DONE block into the Scripts Area.**

5 **Click the Events category and then drag and snap the WHEN GREEN FLAG CLICKED block onto the top of the PLAY SOUND block:**

If you have more than one sound stored in your character sprite, you can choose which one to play by using the drop-down menu in the PLAY SOUND block. Then when you click the Green Flag button, the selected sound should play.

What's the difference between PLAY SOUND and PLAY SOUND UNTIL DONE? If you have more code blocks snapped into place below the PLAY SOUND block, those commands will run *while* the sound is playing. If you use PLAY SOUND UNTIL DONE, the other blocks will *not* run until the sound has finished playing.

If you do not want your sound to play right away, snap a WAIT block above it and set the number of seconds to wait:

ANIMATE CHARACTER SPEECH

If you've recorded dialogue for one of your characters, the next logical step is to make them look like they are speaking. You can achieve this in several ways:

» Display the character while playing the recorded voice. (Duh!)

» Animate the character's mouth. (Easier said than done, right?)

» Show who or what the character is speaking to. (Like how you only see Charlie Brown while some invisible adult is saying, "Whuh wuh wh wh whaughhh.")

» Use a *voiceover,* where you see the character but when he or she starts talking, you show something else. (You often see this in a flashback, where a character tells you about something that already happened while you see some of the stuff he or she is describing.)

» Show an unbearably cute photo of your cat (not!) while we hear your character talking about something completely unrelated to unbearably cute cats.

Aside from the last one, you will see a combination of all these techniques used in animation, sometimes even in the same scene.

In addition to dragging both costumes and code blocks from one sprite to another, you can also drag sounds between sprites. This feature is handy if you ever record audio onto the wrong sprite.

MOUTHING THE WORDS

The more time you are willing to put into animating a character's mouth, the better it is likely to look while speaking. Animators refer to this as *lip-synching*. Synch is short for *synchronization*, which means matching the picture with the sound.

Synching does not have to be hard or too time consuming. I bet you've seen the easy way, where a character's mouth just opens and closes repeatedly while talking and stays closed while *not* talking. A classic hand puppet or marionette works like this.

Did you notice how all the characters I designed in Project 2 start with an open mouth? This lets me add teeth or a tongue or both. Then I can just duplicate the costume and reshape the mouth for the closed-mouth view.

1 **Select the sprite that will be talking, and then click the Costumes tab.**

2 **Shift-click the costume with the character's mouth open and select Duplicate.**

3 **Rename the first costume to *Mouth Open* and the second costume to *Mouth Closed*.**

4 **Select the Mouth Closed costume.**

5 **Use the Reshape tool to modify the mouth so it appears closed.**

You should now have a character sprite with at least two costumes (Mouth Open and Mouth Closed), recorded dialogue, and a short script (two code blocks) that makes the audio play as soon as somebody clicks the Green Flag button.

EASY LIP-SYNCHING

You will use a sequence of code blocks to alternate between the open- and closed-mouth costumes while the audio is playing:

1 **Select the sprite that will be talking, and then click the Scripts tab.**

2 Drag and snap the SWITCH COSTUME TO, WAIT, and REPEAT blocks to the bottom of the other two blocks in the Scripts Area:

I used the drop-down menu to choose Open in one SWITCH COSTUME TO block and Closed in the other. I also changed the WAIT time from the default 1 second to .25 second and the REPEAT value to 8. At the least, you will probably have to tweak the REPEAT value for your character. Can you figure out why?

When the Green Flag button is clicked, I want the mouth to open and close for as *long* as the audio plays. I didn't automatically know it would take 8 times of opening and closing to match the audio. The first time, I guessed 10. That was too long, so I tried 6, and then, finally, 8. You will have to adjust the value based on the length of *your* audio. You can also try different times for the WAIT block until you get the look you want.

 If you do not use the WAIT blocks, the costumes will swap so fast you will not be able to see the costume change.

ACHIEVE MORE REALISTIC LIP-SYNCHING

Go to a mirror, stand really close, fix your gaze on your mouth, and say the word *donut* as slowly as you can. Notice how not only your lips but also your teeth and even your tongue combine in different ways depending on which letters or sounds you are forming. For the *d,* your teeth start together and your tongue is at the roof of your mouth. When you get to *o,* your mouth is open and then it closes partway while your tongue bends up to the roof of your mouth for the *n.* Your mouth opens for the *u* and returns to the same position as the *n* for the *t.*

Don't worry: You do *not* have to draw every single letter of your dialogue (that would take forever)! Most people talk so fast you see only a few distinct mouth shapes. If you don't believe me, go back to that mirror and say, "I love donuts," the way you normally speak.

The key to getting more realistic speaking animation is to animate the shapes the mouth makes at key times, otherwise known as *keyframes* (frames in which something important changes). Animators refer to the basic shapes your mouth makes to form the vowel and consonant sounds as *phonemes.* Although the English alphabet has 26 letters, there are far fewer phonemes because many letters overlap, such as M, P, and B (lips together) and D and T (tongue against upper teeth).

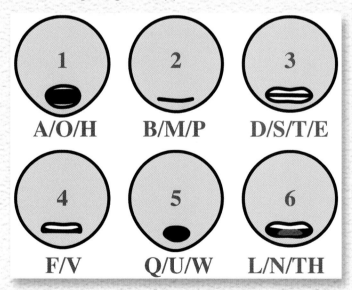

So that you're on the same page as I am, let's all make our characters say, "I love donuts." (I mean, who *doesn't* love donuts?) I'm going to switch to *Zomberta*. Surely, zombies would love those gory jelly donuts if they tried them:

1 **Click the sprite of the character who will be speaking, and then click the Sounds tab.**

2 **Click the Record New Sound button.**

3 **Rename the new sound object** Donuts.

4 **Click the Record button and say, "I love donuts."**

5 **Click the Stop button.**

6 **Select any silence at the beginning of your sound wave and choose Edit ⇨ Delete.**

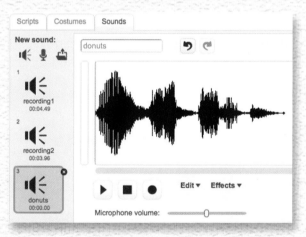

When your donut recording is ready, it is time to choose the key phonemes to add to your character. Here's what I think will work best:

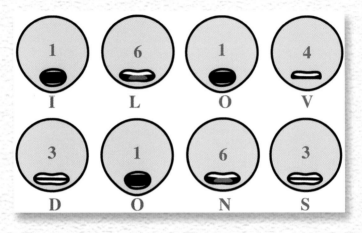

See what I mean about duplicate phonemes (using #1 three times and #3 and #6 twice)? I did not create phonemes for the *u* or the *t* in *donuts*. Can you figure out why? The *t* and *s* are the same phoneme, and when I say *donuts,* the emphasis is on the first syllable ("DO-nuts"), so my mouth barely opens for the *u.*

CREATE CUSTOM PHONEME COSTUMES

You need only phonemes 1, 3, 4, and 6 for your sentence. If you want to use your Mouth Open costume for #1, you need to create just three more mouth shapes:

1 **Select the character you want to animate, and then click the Costumes tab.**

2 **Shift-click the Mouth Open costume and choose Duplicate.**

3 Rename the new costume to correspond to the new phoneme mouth shape you are creating (such as "D/S/T/E").

4 Use the Reshape tool to change the mouth to the desired phoneme shape.

5 Repeat Steps 2–4 for each remaining phoneme.

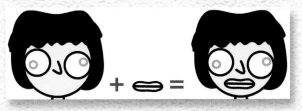

Wanna save yourself a ton of animation time? Why not make a new sprite named Talking, with each phoneme as a different costume. Then you can place that mouth over any character on the Stage. This trick will allow you to animate your character's body separately from its mouth and then duplicate the sprite instead of creating a different set of phonemes for every character.

After you create the phonemes you need, all that's left is to synch them with the audio recording.

SWITCH COSTUMES TO MATCH PHONEMES

Make sure you renamed all your costumes; otherwise, coding will be tricky:

1 Select the sprite containing the phoneme costumes.

2 Click the Scripts tab.

3 Drag the following blocks into the Scripts Area:

4 Shift-click the SWITCH COSTUME TO block, choose Duplicate, and drag and snap the copies to the bottom of the current blocks:

5 Repeat Step 4 until you have a SWITCH COSTUME TO block and a WAIT block for each phoneme.

6 Select the phoneme in each SWITCH COSTUME block.

7 Adjust the values of the WAIT block so the phoneme costumes come at the proper time while playing audio.

My final script looks like this (I added red letters *outside* Scratch to show which blocks correspond to each part of my donuts audio):

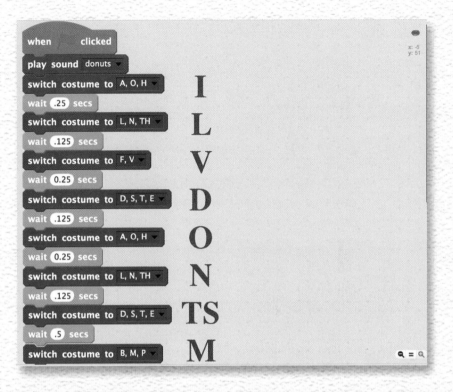

That final *M* shape closes the character's mouth when he or she has finished talking.

After you master the phonemes in *donuts,* you should be able to lip-synch all your animation characters. The key is finding the most important mouth shapes for any given word or phrase. And the faster your character talks, the fewer phonemes you should use. Otherwise, your character's mouth will be moving like crazy!

MORE DIALOGUE TIPS

» **Animate the jaw:** When you speak, it's not just about your lips, teeth, and tongue. Head back to the mirror and see where your jaw is when you go through the phonemes. It's easy to add: Just use the Reshape tool to tweak the bottom of the head.

» **Animate the eyes and eyebrows:** People tend to raise their eyebrows and open their eyes a bit wider when asking a question. What other ways can you change the eyes when a character speaks? (Your mirror beckons.)

» **Add blinking:** Unless your characters are in a staring contest, try adding an occasional blink to make them more realistic (or a wink to get them a date).

» **Animate hands:** Have you noticed how some people move their hands as they speak, almost as if they are conducting an orchestra (or trying to distract you while stealing your wallet)?

» **Try Audacity:** Audacity (audacity.sourceforge.net) is a free audio-editing application that gives you far more control over audio editing than you have with Scratch. Some of the biggest advantages are being able to zoom in to and out of your sound wave, show precise time information, speed up and slow down audio, and apply more sophisticated sound effects.

PROJECT 5 LIGHTS, CAMERA, ACTION!

YOU HAVE COME UP WITH A STORY, CAST YOUR CHARACTERS, CREATED YOUR BACKDROPS, AND RECORDED SOME DIALOGUE. Now it's time to put all the elements together into an animation. The mix of design and programming tips in this project can streamline your animation process.

(NOT) STARTING FROM SCRATCH

You should begin by opening a project that contains any characters, backdrops, or sounds (preferably all three) that you want to include in your animation. I'll be using *my* characters, backdrops, and sounds throughout this project, while you should be using *yours*.

CREATE A NIGHT SCENE

I want my first scene to be an interior of *Hector*'s apartment at night. But what if the character and backdrop I designed look like this:

Does that look like a nighttime scene? It looks like high noon on a sunny day. What could I change to make the scene look like night — and make it more dramatic?

Surely there must be a few Scratch tricks that could save you time changing a bright sunny scene to a dramatic nighttime one, right? For starters, that window is a big giveaway: It should be dark outside. In Project 3, I show you the importance of having back walls as sprites instead of backdrops so you can put other graphics behind the wall, like so:

What if I told you just one code block can make it look even later outside? I will hide *Hector,* his couch, and the wall by Shift-clicking each sprite icon below the Stage and choosing Hide. (I'll unhide them later.)

Some Scratchers don't even think to add code to their backdrop, but several blocks in the Looks category work on backdrops. One of them can help you transform day into night:

1 **Click the Stage button located to the left of your sprite icons.**

2 **Click the Scripts tab.**

3 **Click the Looks category.**

4 **In the Scripts Area, click one time in the SET EFFECT TO block.**

Inside the SET EFFECT TO block, choose Brightness, change the value to **50**, and then click one time in the block. What happens to the backdrop? It gets quite a bit brighter. If you changed the value to the maximum of **100**, the backdrop would be completely white. So how would you make it darker? Try a negative number!

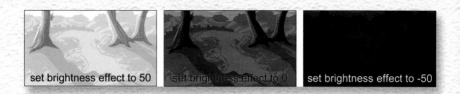

I find −35 works well for my exterior scene. I'll unhide (Shift-click and select Show) the wall, the couch, and *Hector* to see how the scene looks now.

Better. But what if I want it to be darker *inside?*

TURN OUT THE LIGHTS

What if you could put a black curtain over the entire scene and then make it partially transparent? That's where the *Ghost* effect comes in! (**Hint:** It's not just for ghosts.)

1 Below the Stage, click the Paint New Sprite icon.

2 Click the Costumes tab.

3 Click the Fill with Color tool.

4 Click the black color swatch.

5 Click the Solid option to the left of the color swatches.

6 Click the Paint Editor canvas to fill it with black.

7 Click and drag the new sprite to cover the Stage.

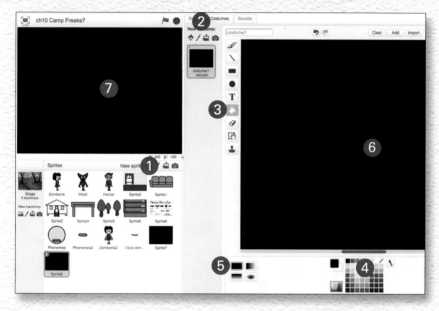

Unless you want complete darkness, you need to drag a SET EFFECT TO block into the new sprite's Scripts Area, along with a WHEN GREEN FLAG CLICKED block. Might as well add a GO TO X Y block, too, and set both values to **0** to ensure that the sprite is centered on the Stage:

When you change the SET EFFECT TO values to **Ghost** and **35** and click the Green Flag button, your scene becomes darker. You can adjust the value to suit your taste.

FADE-IN AND FADE-OUT

You can achieve a fade-in effect at the beginning of a scene by gradually changing the Ghost value from **0** to **100**.

```
set ghost effect to 0
repeat 100
    change ghost effect by 1
```

To fade to black at the end of a scene, set the Ghost value to **100** and change it by **–1**:

```
set ghost effect to 100
repeat 100
    change ghost effect by -1
```

CAMERA (OR WHAT DO I FOCUS ON?)

Have you noticed how animators alternate between wide shots that show you the entire scene and close-ups that may show only part of a character (most frequently, the face)?

In the following three images, I used the SET SIZE TO block to change the size of *Hector,* the window, and the couch from 100% to 250% to 500%:

Wait a minute! Why is there so little difference between the size of *Hector*'s face in the second and third image? Scratch has limitations on how much you can increase a sprite size when using LOOKS blocks. Fortunately, I can make *Hector* even larger in the Paint Editor.

INCREASE THE COSTUME SIZE

You can increase the size of a character's costume by grouping the shapes and using the Grow tool near the very top of the Paint Editor. It is a good idea to duplicate a costume before changing its size so you can quickly switch back to its original size:

1 **Click the Costumes tab.**

2 **Shift-click the current costume and choose** Duplicate.

3 Click the new costume to select it.

4 Change the costume name to zoom in.

5 Click the Select tool.

6 Click and drag across all the shapes in the costume.

7 Click the Group button.

8 Click the Grow tool and click several times on the costume to increase its size.

For interior scenes, you can cheat by filling the costume's background with the wall color (so you do not need to resize other sprites in the scene).

A camera is capable of more than only zooming in and out on characters. Another frequently employed camera technique is to alternate views, such as seeing a character from the front or from the side.

CREATE A BACK VIEW OF CHARACTERS

I ended Project 3 with *Zomberta's* back to the viewer as she appeared to walk toward a camp cabin in the distance.

The following sequence of images shows how I modified the sprite from a front view to a rear view by pulling the hair over her face and then sending her arms to the back layer.

After you have a front and back view for each character, you can alternate between them during an encounter.

If you don't like having a blank wall behind *Zomberta,* you could try flipping the wall sprite so the window appears on the other side.

CREATE A SIDE VIEW OF CHARACTERS

The most frequent use of a side view is for characters walking or running. Here's how you could change *Hector* to a side view by using the Reshape tool:

You can spend days (even weeks) tweaking each character view. Scratch makes it easy to swap costumes later, so don't spend too much time on views until you know your animation really needs each one.

ACTION! (OR LET'S GET THE STORY MOVING)

It is finally time to bring your characters to life, tell your story, and impress your friends, family, and classmates. If you find yourself getting frustrated, check out the credits from any animated film to remind yourself how many people come together to make an animated tale. If you enjoy one part of the process much more than another, perhaps it's time to recruit a few collaborators.

ANIMATE SPRITE ENTERING THE SCENE

To save a bit of time, I'm going to use the "cheap" walking technique, in which a character keeps facing the camera and bounces up and down:

1 Click and drag your sprite to the *ending* position on the Stage (where you want the character to stop once on the Stage).

2 Click the Scripts tab.

3 Drag the following blocks into the Scripts Area and change the values to better fit your sprite and scene:

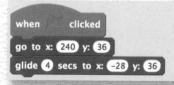

When you click the Green Flag button, you should notice that the character looks like it's being pulled across the floor rather than walking.

ADD A (SLIGHTLY) MORE REALISTIC WALK

When people walk, they do not just move horizontally across the floor. With each step, their entire bodies also move up and down. Replacing that GLIDE block with the following code blocks is a quick way to make your character's walk more believable:

1 Click the Scripts tab for your character's sprite.

2 Delete the GLIDE block below the GO TO X Y block. (Shift-click and choose Delete.)

3 **Drag and snap the following blocks to the bottom of the GO TO block (shown) and change the values to match:**

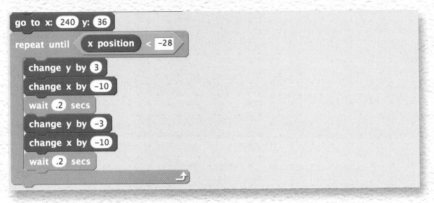

When you click the Green Flag button, your character has a more realistic walk. You can tweak the WAIT values to make your character a bit faster or slower, and change the X and Y values for a better-looking stride.

BROADCAST ANIMATION MESSAGES

When a character reaches its destination, how do you send a message to other sprites and backdrops to do their thing? That's where *broadcasting* comes in!

SEND A BROADCAST MESSAGE

Let me show you how I'd broadcast a message that *Hector* has entered the room to trigger the lightning flash, a sound effect, and the werewolf's sudden appearance:

1 **Click the Scripts tab for your character's sprite, and then click the Events category.**

2 **Drag and snap a BROADCAST AND WAIT block to the bottom of the "walking" blocks (the REPEAT loop you created in the preceding section).**

3 Click Message1 inside the BROADCAST AND WAIT block and choose New Message.

4 Type Lightning and click OK to add a new broadcast message:

The sprite will broadcast the *Lightning* message after it finishes the blocks in the REPEAT loop. But sending a broadcast is only the first part. You need to tell sprites what to do when they *receive* a message.

RECEIVE A BROADCAST MESSAGE

You need to drag a WHEN I RECEIVE block into the Scripts Area for each sprite that you want to react to the broadcast message. When a broadcast message is received, any code blocks attached to the WHEN I RECEIVE block will execute.

Here's how to create a flash of lightning outside the window:

1 Click the Stage button and then click the Scripts tab.

2 Drag the following blocks into the Scripts Area and change the values to match:

You can trigger a sound effect at the same time by snapping a PLAY SOUND block between the WHEN I RECEIVE and the SET BRIGHTNESS EFFECT blocks:

```
when I receive  Lightning ▼
play sound  pop ▼
set  brightness ▼  effect to  50
```

You get the idea? Each event in your story can trigger as many code blocks as you want to use by broadcasting and receiving messages, like a director calling out instructions to actors and technicians during a rehearsal.

SWITCH BETWEEN ANIMATION SCENES

To change scenes in your animation, you need a way to hide sprites that make up your first scene and display sprites that make up your second scene, as well as change any backdrops that may appear.

How do you send a message to hide or show several sprites and change backdrops? This is another ideal use of broadcasting:

1 **Add the following code to each sprite that you want to show at the beginning of your animation and then hide in your second scene:**

```
when   clicked          when I receive  Scene 2 ▼
show                    hide
```

2 In the WHEN I RECEIVE BLOCK, select New Message, type
Scene 2, **and then click OK.**

3 Add the following code to each sprite you want to hide at
the beginning of your animation and show in Scene 2:

```
when   clicked          when I receive  Scene 2 ▼
hide                    show
```

4 If you need to change your backdrop between your
first and second scene, click the Stage icon and add the
following code to the Scripts tab:

```
when I receive  Scene 2 ▼
switch backdrop to  scene 2 backdrop ▼
```

5 In the SWITCH BACKDROP TO block, select the name of
the backdrop you want to use for Scene 2.

Did you notice something missing? You need the block that *sends*
the broadcast message! Where should the BROADCAST block go?
It must go under the last block that executes in Scene 1.

What is the last thing that happens in Scene 1? In my story,
the last thing I coded were the lights going out. So I need the
BROADCAST Scene2 block to go on the Darkness sprite:

```
when   clicked          when I receive  Lights out ▼
hide                    show
                        set  ghost ▼  effect to  35
                        broadcast  Scene 2 ▼
```

It might also be a good idea to add a pause at the end of your scene for dramatic effect by using another BROADCAST or simply a WAIT block.

LEARN MORE ABOUT ANIMATION

The following websites offer tons of tips, techniques, and tutorials to expand your skills.

» www.scratch.mit.edu: Come on, I'm not the only Scratch animator out there (and I'm sure not the best, either!). If you search for animation tutorials, you'll find thousands of projects and hundreds of studios covering a wide range of styles.

» www.youtube.com: On YouTube, you get the best results when you type a specific search. Try searching for "scratch animation tutorial," "simple animation tutorial," or "2d animation tutorial." (If you are in a school that blocks access to YouTube, try www.schooltube.com.)

» www.vimeo.com: Enter the same search terms that you use in YouTube to find many unique tutorials. For example, *The Six Steps of Animation* is a great introduction to more traditional animation techniques that can also be applied to Scratch.

» www.animatorisland.com: An animation community built to share animation techniques from storytelling to drawing to special effects.

» www.jerrysartarama.com/art-lessons/Skill-Level/Kids/: Don't let the long web address scare you off. This site has a bunch of great art and design tutorials.

» diy.org/tags/animation: The online community for kids who like to make stuff, create all kinds of art, learn about the world around them, and experiment with everything from baking to beekeeping.

AND CUT!

The world of animation has so many possibilities. If you go to your favorite library or bookstore, you will find a bunch of books dedicated to animation, from the classic hand-drawn approach to stop-motion and computer animation. In the nearby sidebar, you will find several great resources for inspiration and for expanding your animation skills.

AUTHOR NOTES

THERE IS STILL SO MUCH I HAVEN'T SHARED! Honestly, I've only *scratched* the surface of the programming power in those colorful blocks. But rather than trying to squeeze in one more game project, I'd like to share some important tips for all your Scratch projects.

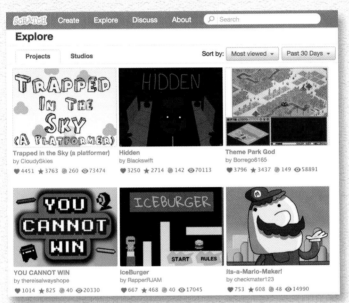

SHARE YOUR SCRATCH PROJECTS IN THE SCRATCH ONLINE COMMUNITY

By default, you are the only person who can see your Scratch projects. To allow other Scratch users to view your project, remix it, or add it to their studio, you must enable sharing. Sharing a project makes it available to all users around the world, so you should delete any personal information or other elements (spare sprites, blocks, and sounds) that you do not want strangers to see. If your project is not yet complete, click the Draft check box before sharing it to inform people that it is a work in process.

SHARE PROJECT FROM THE ONLINE SCRATCH EDITOR

1 Go to www.scratch.mit.edu and log into your account.

2 Click the My Stuff **button near the top-right part of the web page.**

You can tell which projects you have already shared by reading the information on the far right. If a project has not been shared, you will see the option to Delete your project. If it has been shared, you will see the Unshare option.

3 Click the title of the project you want to share.

4 Click the Share button.

5 Fill out the Instructions box and the Notes and Credits box, and choose one to three tags.

SHARE PROJECT FROM THE OFFLINE SCRATCH EDITOR

If you are using the offline Scratch editor, click the File menu and choose Share to Website. You will need to log in with your Scratch account, and then follow Steps 2–5 in the preceding section.

BROADCAST SCRATCH ANIMATION ON ANY WEBSITE

You have seen how sharing a Scratch project will allow logged-in Scratch users to view and remix your projects. You can also display working Scratch projects on your own blog or on another website.

1 Go to www.scratch.mit.edu and log into your account.

2 Click the My Stuff button near the top-right part of the web page.

3 Click the title of the project you want to share on another website.

4 If the project has not yet been shared, click the Share button.

5 Click the Embed button.

6 Select and copy the embed html code.

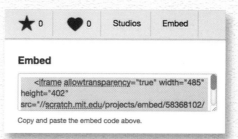

7 Paste the code into your external blog or website.

RECORD/EXPORT SCRATCH VIDEOS

You can record and export a video of your Scratch project, but this feature is currently limited to 60 seconds or less. Depending on what kind of computer you have, you may need to download another program, such as VLC Media Player (www.videolan.org), to play the file. This file will run on YouTube, Vimeo, and Facebook but may need to be converted for other websites such as Twitter and Tumblr:

1 **Open your Scratch project.**

2 **From the Scratch File menu, choose Record Project Video.**

You need to be signed in to see this option.

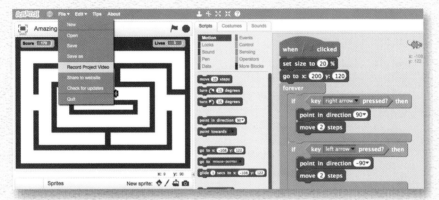

5 **In the More Options menu, choose recording options (such as recording sound and mouse clicks).**

4 **To record the beginning of your project, click the Start button. Or if you want to start recording sometime after the start of the project, click the Green Flag button.**

5 **Click the Stop Recording button (below the Stage).**

After you have recorded for 60 seconds, Scratch stops recording automatically.

6 **Click the Save and Download button to download the file to your computer.**

EXPORT SCRATCH GRAPHICS TO OTHER APPLICATIONS

Once you have mastered bitmap tools, vector tools, and design techniques in the Scratch Paint Editor, wouldn't it be great if you could design graphics for other applications, such as Microsoft Word and PowerPoint? Or what if you just want to be able to print your graphics at any size? An easy-to-find button (Upload from File) allows you to import graphics into Scratch, but many users do not realize that graphics can also be exported. That way, the files can be saved to your computer and then used like any other graphics file.

1 **Open your Scratch project.**

2 **Select one of your sprites.**

3 **Click the Costumes tab.**

4 **Shift-click the costume that has the graphic you want to export and choose Save to Local File.**

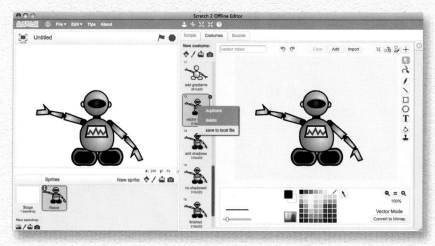

5 **Choose the location where you want to save the file on your computer and then click Save.**

Vector graphics will be saved in SVG format (Scaleable Vector Graphics) and bitmap graphics will be saved in PNG format (Portable Network Graphics). While PNG graphics are supported by most applications, SVG files may need to be converted. (Neither Word nor PowerPoint allow you to import SVG graphics at this time.) Fortunately, you can convert your vector graphics right inside Scratch by clicking the Convert to Bitmap button before you export your costume.

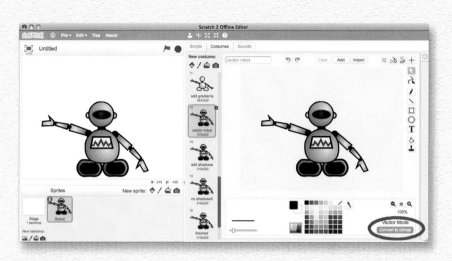

 Zoom your vector costume as much as you can before you click the Convert to Bitmap button to export the maximum resolution image.

DEDICATION

For Dad — thank you for fostering my love of drawing!

ABOUT THE AUTHOR

Derek is the author of *Scratch For Kids* (a *For Dummies* book). He is a founding member of the Instructional Design and Interactive Education Media Association (IDIEM) and is an active member of the Scratch Educator (ScratchEd) community. Most recently, Derek worked as a graphic designer for the StarLogo Nova project at MIT, as a teaching fellow in Instructional Design at Harvard Extension school, and as a curriculum developer for i2 Camp. He is also an ambassador for Europe Code Week (codeweek.eu) and Africa Code Week (africacodeweek.org).

AUTHOR'S ACKNOWLEDGMENTS

Thank you to the editorial staff at Wiley, especially Amy Fandrei and the sensational Susan Pink.

Without the pioneering work of the Lifelong Kindergarten Group at the MIT Media Lab, I would just be scratching my head (and wishing for something like Scratch to fill my head with tinkering ideas). Thank you Mitchel and Natalie and dozens of people who have worked with them on developing Scratch and sustaining the online community.

I am grateful to Daniel Wendel, Wendy Huang, and Josh Sheldon for showing me the true power of blocks-based programming and to Eric Klopfer for hiring me into the StarLogo family.

I am continually inspired by educational technology colleagues in Massachusetts, New York, and beyond, especially Cynthia Solomon, Margaret Minsky, Karen Brennan, Sharon Thompson, Keledy Kenkel, Stephen Lewis, Andrea Meyer, Horst Jens, Martin Wollenberger, Claude Terosier, Joek van Montfort, and Stephen Howell.

The vibrant folks in IDIEM (Instructional Design and Interactive Education Media Association) gave me the confidence to take on this project, especially my good friends Chad Kirchner, Julie Mullen, Diana Ouellette, Ben Mojica, Karen Motley, Jason Alvarez, Jean Devine, and Steve Gordon.

I am also indebted to the fabulous ED103 and ED113 courses at Harvard Extension School, under the masterful direction of Stacie Cassat Green and Denise Snyder.

There would have been far fewer tips and tricks throughout the book were it not for the invaluable Scratch Wiki (www.wiki.scratch.mit.edu) and Scratch Discussion Forums (www.scratch.mit.edu/discuss).

Then there are the Onoratos . . . the Breens . . . the Dowdens . . . the Nangeronis and the Tupelo-Schnecks for ALWAYS being there!

PUBLISHER'S ACKNOWLEDGMENTS

Acquisitions Editor: Amy Fandrei

Project Editor: Susan Pink

Production Editor: Siddique Shaik

Scratch Logo: Courtesy of Mitchel Resnick, Lifelong Kindergarten Group, MIT Media Lab

Chapter figures, illustrations, and Scratch projects: Copyright © 2016 Derek Breen

Scratch is developed by the Lifelong Kindergarten Group at the MIT Media Lab. See http://scratch.mit.edu.